Healthy Cooking

GENERAL EDITOR
CHUCK WILLIAMS

RECIPES
JOHN PHILLIP CARROLL

PHOTOGRAPHY
ALLAN ROSENBERG

TIME
LIFE
BOOKS

TIME-LIFE BOOKS
Time-Life Books is a division of Time Life Inc.
Time-Life is a trademark of Time Warner Inc. U.S.A.

Time-Life Custom Publishing
Vice President and Publisher: Terry Newell
Managing Editor: Donia Ann Steele
Director of Acquisitions: Jennifer L. Pearce
Vice President of Sales and Marketing: Neil Levin
Director of Financial Operations: J. Brian Birky

WILLIAMS-SONOMA
Founder and Vice Chairman: Chuck Williams
Book Buyer: Victoria Kalish

WELDON OWEN INC.
President: John Owen
Vice President and Publisher: Wendely Harvey
Chief Operating Officer: Larry Partington
Vice President International Sales: Stuart Laurence
Managing Editor: Lisa Chaney Atwood
Project Coordinator: Judith Dunham
Consulting Editor: Norman Kolpas
Copy Editor: Sharon Silva
Design: John Bull, The Book Design Company
Production Director: Stephanie Sherman
Production Coordinator: Tarji Mickelson
Production Editor: Janique Gascoigne
Editorial Assistant: Sarah Lemas
Food Photographer: Allan Rosenberg
Additional Food Photography: Allen V. Lott
Primary Food Stylist: Heidi Gintner
Primary Prop Stylist: Sandra Griswold
Assistant Food Stylists: Kim Konecny, Nette Scott
Glossary Illustrations: Alice Harth

The Williams-Sonoma Kitchen Library
conceived and produced by Weldon Owen Inc.
814 Montgomery St., San Francisco, CA 94133

In collaboration with Williams-Sonoma
3250 Van Ness Ave., San Francisco, CA 94109

Printed in Hong Kong by Toppan Printing Co., LTD.

A Note on Weights and Measures:
All recipes include customary U.S. and metric
measurements. Metric conversions are based on
a standard developed for these books and have
been rounded off. Actual weights may vary.

A Weldon Owen Production

Copyright © 1997 Weldon Owen Inc.
Reprinted in 1997; 1997; 1998; 1998; 2000
All rights reserved, including the right of
reproduction in whole or in part in any form.

Library of Congress
Cataloging-in-Publication Data:

Carroll, John Phillip.
    Healthy cooking / general editor, Chuck Williams ;
recipes, John Phillip Carroll ; photography, Allan Rosenberg.
        p.   cm. — (Williams-Sonoma kitchen library)
    ISBN 0-7835-0319-9
    1. Cookery.   2. Low-fat diet—Recipes.   I. Williams, Chuck.
II. Title.   III. Series.
TX714.C3736   1997
641.5'638—dc20   96-24076
                                        CIP

Contents

STARTERS, SOUPS & SALADS 15

MAIN COURSES 33

DESSERTS 85

INTRODUCTION

Too many people who love good food believe they must sacrifice culinary pleasures to have a healthy lifestyle. This book is a response to that mistaken notion. Put simply, it is a guide to preparing everyday fare that both is delicious and fulfills basic nutritional needs.

I want to stress that this is *not* a diet book. It is, instead, a collection of recipes that emphasize freshness, seasonality and variety. Many of the dishes are built on vegetables, fruits and grains, all rich sources of energy-giving complex carbohydrates and filling dietary fiber. Use of butter, oil and cream is kept to a minimum, with most recipes deriving fewer than 30 percent of their calories from fat. All these characteristics contribute to what is commonly recognized as *healthy* eating, an approach to good food that, in combination with regular exercise, is an important part of any thoughtful prescription for long life.

The book begins with some sound advice to help you achieve your own healthier cooking goals, including a guide to essential equipment, a discussion of cooking principles and simple how-to demonstrations of techniques used throughout the book. The 45 recipes that follow are arranged into chapters by courses. Each recipe includes a nutritional analysis to give you a better grasp of how the dish fits into your overall eating plan.

I suggest that you use this book as an aid in planning complete, healthy meals. Enjoy the delectable recipes with your family and friends. Learn the cooking principles behind them. And soon you'll reach that enviable point at which healthy eating becomes part of your daily routine.

Chuck Williams

EQUIPMENT

All-purpose cookware and tools that help you attain the goal of cooking healthier food

Good-quality kitchen equipment will meet the needs of most recipes in this book. Note that many of the stove-top and oven pieces shown have nonstick surfaces that allow cooking with little or no added fat.

1. Large Roasting Pan
Heavy metal pan with high sides for holding sizable roasts and large quantities of other ingredients.

2. Stockpot
Tall, deep, large-capacity pot with close-fitting lid, for making stock, cooking pasta or boiling or steaming large quantities of vegetables. Select a good-quality heavy pot that absorbs and transfers heat well.

3. Saucepan
For making soups, sauces and small quantities of stock, and for cooking vegetables, dried beans and rice.

4. Mixing Bowls
Sturdy bowls in a range of sizes for mixing and serving. Can be made of porcelain, earthenware, glass or stainless steel.

5. Food Mill
Hand-cranked mill purées ingredients by forcing them through its conical grinding disk, which also sieves out fibers, skins and seeds. Some models include both medium and fine disks for coarser or smoother purées.

6. Large Roasting Pan
Metal pan for roasting vegetables and baking pastas and casseroles.

7. Cake Pan
Standard 8-inch (20-cm) square pan for baking cakes and fruit desserts. Choose heavy aluminum or tinplate steel, which conducts heat well for fast, even baking.

8. Fine-Mesh Sieve
For straining stocks, draining the liquid from yogurt to make yogurt cheese and other general uses. Select a sturdy stainless-steel model with a securely attached handle, a wire-mesh bowl and a hook for gripping the lip of a mixing bowl.

9. Soufflé Dish
For molding both cold and hot soufflés and for general serving use.

10. Baking Sheet
For making toasts and roasting peppers.

11. Liquid Measuring Cup
For accurate measuring of liquid ingredients. Choose heavy-duty heat-resistant glass, marked on one side in cups and ounces, on the other in milliliters.

12. Dutch Oven or Casserole
Large-capacity enameled metal cooking vessel with tight-fitting ovenproof lid

holds stews, braises and a variety of foods for baking.

13. Tube Pan
Cake pan with center tube conducts heat so angel food and other cakes bake evenly.

14. Frying Pan
For all-purpose panfrying, sautéing and stir-frying. Choose good-quality heavy aluminum, stainless steel, cast iron or enameled steel.

15. Baking Dishes
Medium-sized rectangular dishes for holding small roasts and baked dishes.

16. Assorted Utensils
Stainless-steel jar holds metal spoon for stirring and basting; slotted metal spoon for removing pieces of food from cooking liquids; wooden spoon for all-purpose stirring; wire whisk for stirring sauces and beating egg whites; rubber spatula for folding ingredients into cake batters and other mixtures; basting brush; ladle for serving soups and other liquid or moist preparations; metal spatula, metal tongs and two-pronged fork for turning foods during cooking; and instant-read thermometer for inserting at the earliest moment a roast might be done for a quick, accurate reading.

17. Pie Pan
For molding polenta and other preparations and for baking pies. Some pans have tiny holes in bottom to ensure even browning of the crust.

18. Colander
For straining solids from stock or draining other ingredients from their cooking liquids.

19. Kitchen Shears
For cutting up poultry and for other heavy-duty kitchen cutting purposes.

20. Zester
Small, sharp holes at end of stainless-steel blade cut citrus zest into fine shreds.

21. Vegetable Peeler
Curved, slotted blade thinly strips away vegetable peels. Choose a sturdy model that feels comfortable in your hand.

22. Corer
Cylindrical blade with serrated edge cuts down vertically through an apple or pear to remove core while leaving fruit whole.

23. Utility Knife and Chef's Knife
Small knife for peeling vegetables, cutting up small ingredients and all-purpose trimming. Larger knife for chopping and slicing large items or large quantities of ingredients. Select knives with sharp stainless-steel blades securely attached to sturdy handles that feel comfortable in the hand.

24. Dry Measuring Cups
For precise measuring of dry ingredients. Choose a set in graduated sizes, with straight rims for easy leveling.

25. Measuring Spoons
Calibrated metal spoons with deep bowls for measuring small quantities of ingredients.

26. Cutting Board
Choose board of hardwood or tough but resilient white acrylic. Thoroughly clean after every use.

Healthy Cooking Basics

A brief survey of the nutritional principles behind healthy cooking, and some strategies for following them

There is no mystery to healthy cooking. All it requires is that you keep in mind a few principles of healthy *eating* and adapt basic cooking methods accordingly. The following paragraphs explain those principles, and the techniques demonstrated on pages 10–11 show how easy it is to put them into practice.

Principles of Healthy Eating

A healthy regimen is one that includes all the nutrients your body needs to function well. Nutritionists agree that most of our daily calories—at least 55 percent—should come from complex carbohydrates such as whole grains, pastas, starchy vegetables and beans. These foods also provide rich amounts of dietary fiber, which should be consumed at the level of 20–35 grams daily for good health. Another 15 percent of our calories should come from lean animal or vegetable protein—about 6 ounces (185 g) seafood, poultry or meat per day for the average person. (Each gram of carbohydrate or protein is equivalent to 4 calories.) No more than 30 percent of our daily calories should derive from fat, and no more than one-third of that fat should be from animal sources or tropical oils, which may contain and also increase the body's own production of cholesterol.

One final consideration is sodium, both present naturally in foods and added to recipes through salt. Although nutritionists believe we should consume between 1,100 and 3,300 milligrams of sodium daily, most people eat too much of it. Some people are genetically predisposed to retain sodium, a trait that can lead to high blood pressure and calls for a sodium-restricted diet. Check with your doctor to find out if you fall into this category.

Daily menus composed of recipes in this book will meet the healthy eating guidelines outlined here (see the sidebar at right for an explanation of the nutritional analysis that accompanies each recipe). They will also help provide the essential vitamins and minerals that the body needs to function at peak efficiency.

Making Healthy Food Choices

With these principles in mind, it is easy to cook more healthily. Begin by planning meals in advance around seasonal produce. Shop at greengrocers that are known to have the widest range of high-quality fruits and vegetables, or find local farmers' markets that offer greater variety and freshness and better value than conventional food stores. Such markets, as well as health-food stores, are also good sources for buying whole grains and dried beans in bulk. Store them at home in airtight containers, ready to be transformed into high-carbohydrate, high-fiber, protein-rich, low-fat dishes.

Since a healthy diet requires only about half the protein most people eat in a day, consider seafood, poultry and meat as playing a supporting role in your meals, rather than as featured ingredients. Shop with an eye toward reducing the dietary fat that is naturally present in animal protein, opting whenever possible for seafood, skinless white-meat poultry and the leanest cuts of red meat.

CUTTING OUT THE FAT

When cooking, find ways to eliminate the fat present in ingredients, and add as little fat as possible. Strip away and discard poultry skin, before or after cooking depending upon the recipe. Use nonstick cookware, which requires little or no fat or oil, and coat cooking surfaces with nonstick spray when possible. If a sauté recipe requires a little fat for browning, pour it from the pan before proceeding with the next step. When cooking tender ingredients such as shrimp (prawns), opt for grilling or broiling. Both methods allow fat to drip away from food, with healthier results.

READING A NUTRITIONAL CHART

A chart accompanying every recipe provides an analysis of the significant nutrients per serving. Calculated by a registered dietitian, these computations can be used to work toward your own healthy eating goals.

Among the figures listed are those for total fat, saturated fat and cholesterol. Remember that total fat should account for no more than 30 percent of total daily calories (1 gram of fat is equivalent to 9 calories) or kilojoules (a term used instead of calories in some countries; 1 calorie is equal to 4.2 kilojoules). At the same time, saturated fat, because it is believed to raise blood cholesterol, should amount to no more than one-third of the total fat calories. Daily intake of cholesterol, a substance present only in animal products, ideally should fall below 300 milligrams.

Each analysis is based on the specific ingredients listed for the recipe. Not included are items listed as "optional"; added "to taste"; suggested as a substitution or accompaniment in a recipe introduction; or shown in a food photograph. If you are on a sodium-restricted diet, bear in mind that 1 teaspoon regular salt adds 2,200 milligrams of sodium and 1 teaspoon coarse, kosher or sea salt adds 1,800 milligrams. Black or white pepper added to taste will not alter nutritional values.

NUTRITIONAL ANALYSIS
PER SERVING:

CALORIES 385
(KILOJOULES 1,617)
PROTEIN 26 G
CARBOHYDRATES 47 G
TOTAL FAT 10 G
SATURATED FAT 2 G
CHOLESTEROL 48 MG
SODIUM 250 MG
DIETARY FIBER 2 G

Healthy Cooking Methods

The four cooking methods demonstrated here, as well as other techniques used in the recipes throughout this book, offer low-fat ways to intensify the flavor and safeguard or enhance the moistness of fresh ingredients.

Panfrying

The quantity of oil or butter commonly required for panfrying is significantly reduced by using a nonstick frying pan coated with nonstick cooking spray.

Sealing in juices.
Meat, poultry and fish—here, salmon fillets—retain their juices and acquire a flavorful, well-browned surface when rapidly panfried over medium to high heat. Lively seasonings such as a low-fat marinade or sauce help add moisture and enrich taste.

Roasting

A minimum of added fat—only a thin coating of nonstick cooking spray on a roasting pan—is needed to oven-cook meat, poultry, fish and vegetables.

Enhancing flavor.
Roasting foods in the dry heat of an oven intensifies their taste, and basting during cooking preserves their moisture. A low-fat, carbohydrate-rich stuffing is a healthy way to add flavor to lean cuts of meat—here, turkey breast.

Braising

Gentle cooking in stock or other well-seasoned liquid, with only a small amount of added fat, yields tender, succulent meat, poultry, fish and vegetables.

Slow cooking for added flavor.
For the braising liquid, aromatic vegetables are sautéed, then simmered in stock to bring out their flavors. Main ingredients that need longer cooking—here, fennel bulbs—are added to the liquid first.

Grilling and Broiling

Searing heat draws fat away from grilled or broiled foods while locking in flavor and moisture. Marinades and basting liquids enhance the results.

Selecting and preparing foods.
Large cuts of meat and poultry, pieces of firm-fleshed fish and sturdy vegetables are set directly on the grill or broiler rack. Small or tender foods—here, shrimp (prawns)—are easier to handle when threaded on skewers.

Salmon Fillets with Chive Sauce

Roasted Vegetable Stock

Making your own vegetable stock is worth the effort because the result is fresher tasting than canned or powdered alternatives. The longer you roast the vegetables, the darker and more strongly flavored the stock will be.

7 large carrots, unpeeled, cut into chunks
3 yellow onions, unpeeled, quartered
8 celery stalks, cut into chunks
½ lb (250 g) fresh mushrooms with stems intact, brushed clean and quartered
1 large baking potato, unpeeled, cut into chunks
2 cups (16 fl oz/500 ml) plus 4½ qt (4.5 l) water
4–6 fresh thyme or parsley sprigs, or a mixture
¼ teaspoon whole peppercorns, crushed
1 bay leaf

Preheat an oven to 350°F (180°C). Coat a large roasting pan with nonstick cooking spray.

Spread the carrots, onions, celery, mushrooms and potato in the pan. Roast for 45 minutes to 1 hour, or for up to 1½ hours if you want a more strongly flavored stock, stirring once or twice.

Remove from the oven and transfer the vegetables to a large stockpot. Add the 2 cups (16 fl oz/500 ml) water to the roasting pan, then stir and scrape the bottom with a spatula to remove any browned bits. Add to the stockpot along with the 4½ qt (4.5 l) water, thyme and/or parsley, peppercorns and bay leaf. Bring to a boil over high heat, skimming off any scum from the surface. Reduce the heat to low, cover partially and simmer for 2 hours.

Strain the stock through a sieve or colander into a large bowl. Discard the solids. Let the stock cool, then store in the refrigerator for up to 4 days or in the freezer for up to 3 months.

Makes about 4 qt (4 l)

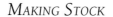

MAKING STOCK

Any stock, whether made from vegetables, shown here, or from seafood, poultry or meat, relies on slow simmering to draw out the essence of the featured ingredients into the water. In some instances, these ingredients are first roasted or otherwise browned to intensify their flavors.

1. Roasting the vegetables. Evenly arrange chunks of vegetables in a large roasting pan coated with nonstick spray. Roast until well browned on all sides. Stir during roasting with a spatula or spoon to ensure even cooking.

2. Skimming the stock. Bring the vegetables, water and seasonings to a boil. As impurities rise to the surface in the form of froth or scum, use a ladle or large metal spoon to skim them off and discard.

3. Straining the stock. Place a colander or sieve inside a large mixing bowl. Ladle the contents of the pot into the colander or sieve to strain out the solids. Lift out the colander or sieve and discard the solids. Let the stock cool at room temperature.

Yogurt Cheese

Yogurt cheese is firmer and creamier than yogurt because much of the water has been drained off. Use it to top baked potatoes and fresh or cooked fruits. It's also an excellent spread for toast and bagels. Check well-stocked food stores for yogurt without stabilizers. Yogurt with such additives cannot be drained as thoroughly.

4 cups (2 lb/1 kg) nonfat plain yogurt *(see note)*

Without stirring the yogurt, gently spoon it into a fine-mesh sieve set over a bowl. Don't worry about the small amount of yogurt that will ooze through the holes. If you have only a sieve with large holes, line it with cheesecloth (muslin) first. Let the yogurt drain, in the refrigerator, for about 8 hours or for as long as overnight. Discard the liquid in the bowl. The yogurt remaining in the sieve is yogurt cheese.

Store in a tightly covered container in the refrigerator for up to 1 week.

Makes 2–2½ cups (1–1¼ lb/500–625 g)

Yogurt and Herb Dressing

The pleasing tang of a yogurt dressing lends itself to a variety of salad greens and cold cooked vegetables. For a creamier dressing, substitute a few tablespoons of mayonnaise, either reduced-fat or regular, for part of the yogurt.

1 cup (8 oz/250 g) low-fat plain yogurt
3 tablespoons white wine vinegar or cider vinegar
1 teaspoon salt
pinch of freshly ground pepper
2 tablespoons chopped fresh dill, tarragon, parsley
   or chives

In a small bowl, combine the yogurt, vinegar, salt, pepper and herb of choice. Using a whisk or fork, stir until blended and smooth.

Store in a tightly capped jar in the refrigerator for up to 3 days.

Makes about 1¼ cups (10 fl oz/310 ml)

Honey Mustard Dressing

Sweet, with a hot and spicy edge, this creamy dressing is good on fruit salads and on sturdy greens such as iceberg or romaine (cos) lettuce.

⅔ cup (5 oz/155 g) low-fat plain yogurt
¼ cup (3 oz/90 g) honey
2 tablespoons Dijon mustard
2 tablespoons water
½ teaspoon salt
pinch of freshly ground pepper

*I*n a small bowl, combine the yogurt, honey, mustard, water, salt and pepper. Using a whisk or fork, stir until blended and smooth.

 Store in a tightly capped jar in the refrigerator for up to 3 days.

Makes about 1¼ cups (10 fl oz/310 ml)

Orange Marmalade– Raspberry Sauce

Spoon this colorful fruit sauce over sherbets or ices, sliced peaches or pears, or the cold raspberry-yogurt soufflé on page 102.

3 cups (12 oz/375 g) raspberries
½ cup (5 oz/155 g) orange marmalade
1 tablespoon finely grated orange zest
2 tablespoons sugar
2 tablespoons orange liqueur, optional

*I*n a food processor fitted with the metal blade or in a blender, combine the raspberries and marmalade and purée until smooth. Strain the mixture through a fine-mesh sieve to remove the seeds. It is difficult to remove every seed, so don't worry if a few make their way into the sauce. Stir in the orange zest, the sugar and the orange liqueur, if using.

 Store in a tightly covered container in the refrigerator for up to 5 days.

Makes about 1¼ cups (10 fl oz/310 ml)

Asparagus and Red Pepper Salad

4 large red bell peppers (capsicums),
   roasted, peeled and cut lengthwise
   into strips about ¼ inch (6 mm)
   wide *(see glossary, page 104)*
2 tablespoons red or white wine vinegar
1 tablespoon Dijon mustard
2 tablespoons chopped fresh tarragon
   or ½ teaspoon dried tarragon
salt and freshly ground pepper
1 lb (500 g) asparagus (16–20 spears)
4 fresh tarragon, parsley or watercress
   sprigs

Green asparagus spears contrast with bright red pepper strips in this springtime salad, which makes a fitting first course for an elegant supper. Offer it as a prelude to a roast chicken or a baked pasta, such as the baked penne with eggplant, summer squash and tomatoes on page 52.

*T*o make the dressing, in a food processor fitted with the metal blade or in a blender, combine ½ cup (3 oz/90 g) of the pepper strips with the vinegar and mustard. Purée until smooth. Add the tarragon and season to taste with salt and pepper.

   Toss ¼ cup (2 fl oz/60 ml) of the dressing with the remaining pepper strips. Set aside both the pepper strips and the remaining dressing.

   Cut or snap off the tough, pale, fibrous bottoms from the asparagus spears. If the spears are especially large, peel the tough skin: Using a vegetable peeler and starting about halfway down from the tip, peel away the thin outer skin. Choose a frying pan large enough to hold the asparagus flat and fill three-fourths full of water. Bring to a boil, add the asparagus spears and boil until just tender, 3–5 minutes; the timing will depend upon the size of the spears. Drain, pat dry with paper towels and let cool.

   To serve, spread the asparagus on a platter or divide among individual plates. Top with the dressed pepper strips. Spoon the remaining dressing over the asparagus and pepper strips. Garnish with the herb or watercress sprigs and serve.

Serves 4

Nutritional Analysis Per Serving:

Calories 52
(Kilojoules 218)
Protein 4 g
Carbohydrates 10 g
Total Fat 0 g
Saturated Fat 0 g
Cholesterol 0 mg
Sodium 94 mg
Dietary Fiber 3 g

15

Curried Leek and Apple Soup

4 large leeks
1 tablespoon unsalted butter
3 large apples such as Golden Delicious,
    pippin or Granny Smith, peeled, cored
    and cut into ½-inch (12-mm) dice
1 cup (4 oz/125 g) thinly sliced celery
2 teaspoons curry powder
4 cups (32 fl oz/1 l) roasted vegetable
    stock *(recipe on page 11)* or low-
    sodium chicken broth
1 small baking potato, peeled and cut
    into ½-inch (12-mm) dice
½ cup (4 fl oz/125 ml) low-fat milk
salt and freshly ground pepper

This fragrant, savory soup makes excellent cold-weather fare.

Cut off all but about 2 inches (5 cm) of the green tops of the leeks; reserve 4–6 thin slices of the tender portion of the green tops for garnish, if desired. Slit each leek lengthwise to within about 2 inches (5 cm) of the root end and rinse well under running water to dislodge any dirt trapped between the leaves. Trim the root end and thinly slice each leek crosswise.

In a large saucepan over medium-low heat, melt the butter. When hot, add the apples, celery, curry powder and leeks and stir well. Cook, stirring occasionally, until the leeks soften, about 5 minutes. Cover the pan and cook for 5 minutes longer, stirring once at the halfway point.

Add the stock or broth and potato and bring to a boil over medium-high heat. Reduce the heat to low, cover and simmer until the apples and potatoes are tender when pierced with a knife, about 20 minutes.

Working in batches, ladle the soup into a blender or into a food processor fitted with the metal blade and purée until smooth. Alternatively, pass the soup through a food mill.

If serving the soup hot, return it to the pan and stir in the milk. Season to taste with salt and pepper. Reheat over low heat without boiling, then ladle into warmed bowls. Garnish with the leek tops, if using, and serve at once.

If serving the soup cold, transfer it to a bowl or other container, stir in the milk and season to taste with salt and pepper. Cover and refrigerate, stirring it every hour or so, until thoroughly chilled, 4–6 hours. When ready to serve, taste and adjust the seasonings, then ladle into chilled bowls, garnish with the leek tops, if using, and serve at once.

Makes about 7 cups (56 fl oz/1.75 l); serves 6

Nutritional Analysis Per Serving:

Calories 174
(Kilojoules 731)
Protein 3 g
Carbohydrates 36 g
Total Fat 3 g
Saturated Fat 2 g
Cholesterol 7 mg
Sodium 60 mg
Dietary Fiber 5 g

Corn Pancakes with Fresh Tomato Salsa

1½ cups (9 oz/270 g) corn kernels

1 whole egg, plus 1 egg white

⅔ cup (5 fl oz/160 ml) buttermilk

dash of hot-pepper sauce

⅔ cup (3 oz/90 g) all-purpose (plain) flour

½ teaspoon salt

½ teaspoon baking powder

¼ teaspoon baking soda (bicarbonate of soda)

2 tablespoons chopped fresh parsley

½ cup (4 fl oz/125 ml) fresh tomato salsa *(see note)*

½ cup (4 oz/125 g) yogurt cheese *(recipe on page 12)* or nonfat plain yogurt

NUTRITIONAL ANALYSIS PER SERVING:

CALORIES 197
(KILOJOULES 827)
PROTEIN 10 G
CARBOHYDRATES 34 G
TOTAL FAT 3 G
SATURATED FAT 1 G
CHOLESTEROL 55 MG
SODIUM 519 MG
DIETARY FIBER 3 G

Serve these corn-flecked pancakes as a brunch or lunch main dish, or as a side dish with meat or poultry. Look for fresh tomato salsa in the refrigerator case of well-stocked food stores.

In a blender or in a food processor fitted with the metal blade, combine 1 cup (6 oz/180 g) of the corn kernels with the whole egg and egg white, buttermilk, hot-pepper sauce, flour, salt, baking powder and baking soda. Process until the batter is blended and smooth, about 30 seconds, stopping once to scrape down the sides of the container. Scrape the batter into a bowl and stir in the parsley and the remaining ½ cup (3 oz/90 g) corn.

Coat a large nonstick frying pan with nonstick cooking spray and place over medium heat. When the pan is hot— the batter should sizzle when it hits the surface—spoon in about 2 tablespoons batter for each pancake. Do not crowd the pan. Cook the pancakes on the first side until they are dry around the edges and a few small bubbles appear on the surface, about 2 minutes. Using a spatula, turn carefully and cook until lightly browned and dry on the second side, 1–1½ minutes longer. Transfer to a warmed platter and cover loosely with aluminum foil to keep warm until all the pancakes are cooked.

Serve the pancakes at once. Pass the salsa and the yogurt cheese or yogurt at the table.

Makes about sixteen 3-inch (7.5-cm) pancakes; serves 4

Tuscan Tomato Salad

5 ripe tomatoes, peeled (*see glossary, page 107*)

2 cloves garlic, minced

1 teaspoon salt

pinch of freshly ground pepper

2 tablespoons balsamic vinegar or red wine vinegar

3 tablespoons olive oil

6 oz (185 g) French or Italian bread (not sourdough), about ½ loaf, with crusts intact

2 cups (2 oz/60 g) fresh curly-leaf parsley sprigs or 1 cup (1 oz/30 g) fresh flat-leaf (Italian) parsley sprigs

½ cup (½ oz/15 g) fresh basil leaves, torn into small pieces, optional

The ingredients for this salad may seem humble, but the result is delectable! An adaptation of a traditional Italian salad, it is a fine way of using leftover or day-old—but not stale—bread.

Cut the tomatoes in half crosswise. Working over a sieve set in a bowl, gently squeeze each half to force out the seed sacs and release the juice. Discard the seeds in the strainer. Put the tomatoes in the bowl with their juice and break up and mash slightly with your fingers or a fork. Add the garlic, salt, pepper, vinegar and oil. Toss gently but thoroughly to combine and coat the ingredients.

Cut or tear the bread into 1-inch (2.5-cm) pieces. Add the bread and parsley and the basil, if using, to the bowl and toss until the bread is moistened but not soggy. Serve at once.

Serves 4

NUTRITIONAL ANALYSIS
PER SERVING:

CALORIES 246
(KILOJOULES 1,033)
PROTEIN 5 G
CARBOHYDRATES 31 G
TOTAL FAT 12 G
SATURATED FAT 2 G
CHOLESTEROL 0 MG
SODIUM 829 MG
DIETARY FIBER 4 G

Carrot and Watercress Soup

1 tablespoon vegetable oil

6 large carrots, 1 lb (500 g) total weight, peeled and cut into 1-inch (2.5-cm) pieces

1 yellow onion, thinly sliced

½ cup (2 oz/60 g) thinly sliced celery

3 fresh parsley sprigs

1 teaspoon chopped fresh thyme or ¼ teaspoon dried thyme

4 cups (32 fl oz/1 l) roasted vegetable stock *(recipe on page 11)* or low-sodium chicken broth

1 slice good-quality white sandwich bread, torn into pieces

1½ cups (2½ oz/70 g) chopped watercress leaves

salt and freshly ground pepper

An appealing color, a delicate sweetness and the subtle peppery flavor of watercress combine to make this soup memorable. You can add 1 cup (3 oz/90 g) thinly sliced green (spring) onion tops in place of the watercress. The soup is delicious hot or chilled.

*I*n a large saucepan over medium-low heat, warm the oil. When hot, add the carrots, onion, celery, parsley and thyme and cook, stirring occasionally, until the vegetables have softened slightly and the onion has wilted, about 5 minutes. Add ¼ cup (2 fl oz/60 ml) of the stock or broth; cover and cook for 5 minutes more, stirring once at the halfway point.

Add the remaining 3¾ cups (30 fl oz/940 ml) stock or broth and the bread and bring to a boil over medium-high heat. Reduce the heat to low, cover and simmer until the carrots are very tender when pierced with the tip of a sharp knife, 20–25 minutes.

Working in batches, ladle the soup into a blender or into a food processor fitted with the metal blade and purée until smooth. Alternatively, pass the soup through a food mill.

If serving the soup hot, return it to the pan and stir in the watercress. Season to taste with salt and pepper. Reheat over low heat without boiling, then ladle into warmed bowls and serve at once.

If serving the soup cold, transfer it to a bowl or other container, stir in the watercress and season to taste with salt and pepper. Cover and refrigerate, stirring it every hour or so, until thoroughly chilled, 4–6 hours. When ready to serve, taste and adjust the seasonings, then ladle into chilled bowls and serve at once.

Makes about 6 cups (48 fl oz/1.5 l); serves 4

Nutritional Analysis Per Serving:

Calories 130
(Kilojoules 546)
Protein 3 g
Carbohydrates 22 g
Total Fat 4 g
Saturated Fat 1 g
Cholesterol 0 mg
Sodium 104 mg
Dietary Fiber 6 g

Artichoke Heart and Orzo Salad

2½ qt (2.5 l) water

⅓ cup (3 fl oz/80 ml) fresh lemon juice, plus the juice of 1 lemon

14–16 baby artichokes, about 1 lb (500 g) total weight

½ lb (250 g) orzo or other rice-shaped pasta

2 tablespoons olive oil

¼ cup (1½ oz/45 g) roasted, peeled and diced red bell pepper (capsicum) (see glossary, page 104)

2 tablespoons Dijon mustard

2 tablespoons white wine vinegar

2 tablespoons chopped fresh tarragon or parsley or ½ teaspoon dried tarragon

salt and freshly ground pepper

This pasta salad takes well to several additions, including cooked shrimp (prawns) or scallops, or neatly cut leftover vegetables.

Combine the water and the ⅓ cup (3 fl oz/80 ml) lemon juice in a large saucepan and bring to a rolling boil over high heat. Have ready a bowl of water to which you have added the juice of 1 lemon.

Meanwhile, working with 1 artichoke at a time, pull off and discard the tough outer leaves, removing two or three layers until you reach the more tender yellow-green leaves. Cut off about 1 inch (2.5 cm) from the top to remove the thorns and tough tips of the leaves. Cut off the stem end even with the bottom. Cut the trimmed artichokes into halves or quarters, depending upon their size. The pieces should be about ½ inch (12 mm) thick. As each artichoke is finished, drop it into the bowl of lemon water.

Drain the artichoke pieces and add them and the orzo to the boiling water. Boil until the orzo is *al dente* (tender but firm to the bite) and the artichokes are tender when pierced with the tip of a sharp knife, 8–10 minutes. Drain the artichokes and orzo well and place in a large bowl. Add the olive oil and, using a fork, toss to coat evenly. Let cool, stirring and tossing occasionally.

Meanwhile, in a small bowl, combine the roasted pepper, mustard, vinegar and tarragon or parsley. Using a fork, stir to combine. Add to the orzo mixture and stir and toss to coat the ingredients evenly. Season to taste with salt and pepper. Serve at once.

Serves 4

NUTRITIONAL ANALYSIS
PER SERVING:

CALORIES 307
(KILOJOULES 1,289)
PROTEIN 9 G
CARBOHYDRATES 48 G
TOTAL FAT 8 G
SATURATED FAT 1 G
CHOLESTEROL 0 MG
SODIUM 237 MG
DIETARY FIBER 4 G

Chick-pea Soup with Pita Toasts

1 cup (7 oz/220 g) dried chick-peas (garbanzo beans) or 3 cups (21 oz/ 655 g) drained canned chick-peas

FOR THE PITA TOASTS:
3 pita breads, whole wheat (wholemeal) or plain
3 teaspoons olive oil
3 tablespoons freshly grated Parmesan cheese
salt and freshly ground pepper

FOR THE SOUP:
1 tablespoon olive oil
½ cup (2 oz/60 g) chopped shallots or green (spring) onions
½ cup (2 oz/60 g) thinly sliced carrot
½ cup (2 oz/60 g) thinly sliced celery
½ cup (1½ oz/45 g) thinly sliced fresh mushrooms
5 cups (40 fl oz/1.25 l) roasted vege-table stock (recipe on page 11) or low-sodium chicken broth
1 teaspoon dried thyme
salt and freshly ground pepper
fresh thyme leaves, optional

NUTRITIONAL ANALYSIS
PER SERVING:
CALORIES 291
(KILOJOULES 1,222)
PROTEIN 12 G
CARBOHYDRATES 45 G
TOTAL FAT 8 G
SATURATED FAT 2 G
CHOLESTEROL 2 MG
SODIUM 262 MG
DIETARY FIBER 6 G

If using dried chick-peas, pick over the chick-peas, discarding any impurities and damaged peas. Rinse, drain and place in a bowl with water to cover by 2 inches (5 cm). Let soak for about 8 hours or overnight. Drain and place in a saucepan with water to cover by 2 inches (5 cm). Bring to a boil, reduce the heat to low, cover partially and simmer until tender, 2–2½ hours. Drain and set aside. If using canned chick-peas, rinse in cold water, drain well and set aside.

Meanwhile, to make the toasts, preheat an oven to 400°F (200°C). Prick one side of each pita bread in several places with a fork, then brush with 1 teaspoon of the olive oil. Cut each round into 4 equal wedges and place on an ungreased baking sheet. Sprinkle with the Parmesan cheese, then season lightly with salt and pepper. Bake until crisp and golden, about 12 minutes. Transfer to a rack to cool. If the toasts soften, recrisp them in a 400°F (200°C) oven for a minute or two.

To make the soup, in a large saucepan over medium-low heat, warm the oil. When hot, add the shallots or green onions, carrot, celery and mushrooms. Cook gently, stirring frequently, until the vegetables have softened slightly, about 5 minutes. Add the stock or broth, dried thyme and reserved chick-peas; bring to a boil over medium-high heat. Reduce the heat to low, cover and simmer until the vegetables and chick-peas are very soft, about 40 minutes.

Working in batches, ladle the soup into a blender or into a food processor fitted with the metal blade and purée until smooth. Alternatively, pass the soup through a food mill. Return the soup to the pan and season to taste with salt and pepper.

Reheat over low heat without boiling, then ladle into warmed bowls and garnish with fresh thyme leaves, if desired. Serve at once with the pita toasts.

Makes about 8 cups (64 fl oz/2 l); serves 6

Grapefruit, Black Olive and Mint Salad

2 large grapefruits, preferably pink or
   Ruby Red
1 cup (1 oz/30 g) fresh mint leaves,
   stems removed
½ cup (2½ oz/75 g) sliced black olives
2 tablespoons olive oil
1 teaspoon fresh lemon juice
¼ teaspoon salt
several leaves of butter (Boston) lettuce
   or iceberg lettuce

The idea for this unusual salad comes from cookbook author Marion Cunningham. If you can't envision the unlikely combination, you're in for a treat. It complements a main course of fish or chicken.

Using a small, sharp knife, cut a slice off the top and the bottom of each grapefruit, cutting deeply enough to expose the fruit. Then, place each grapefruit upright on a cutting board and thickly slice off the peel in strips, removing all of the white pith and exposing the flesh all around. Working over a sieve set in a large bowl, and using a small, sharp knife, remove the grapefruit sections by cutting them away from the membrane, first on one side of each section and then on the other. Let the whole sections fall into the sieve. Remove any seeds and discard.

Pour off any juice in the bowl and reserve for another use (it makes a refreshing drink). In the bowl, combine the grapefruit sections, mint leaves, olives, olive oil, lemon juice and salt. Toss gently to combine, taking care not to break the grapefruit sections.

To serve, line a platter or individual plates with the lettuce leaves and spoon the grapefruit mixture on top. Serve at once.

Serves 4

*Nutritional Analysis
Per Serving:*

Calories 122
(Kilojoules 512)
Protein 1 g
Carbohydrates 11 g
Total Fat 9 g
Saturated Fat 1 g
Cholesterol 0 mg
Sodium 290 mg
Dietary Fiber 1 g

Spinach and Pear Salad

FOR THE VINEGAR-MUSTARD DRESSING:

2 tablespoons fruit vinegar (preferably raspberry) or balsamic vinegar

1 tablespoon Dijon mustard

1 tablespoon walnut oil or olive oil

2 teaspoons sugar

salt and freshly ground pepper

FOR THE CHUTNEY DRESSING:

¼ cup (2½ oz/75 g) mango or peach chutney

¼ cup (2 oz/60 g) low-fat plain yogurt

8 cups (8 oz/250 g) loosely packed spinach leaves (*see note*)

2 firm, ripe pears such as Bosc or Bartlett (Williams')

Here is a satisfying winter salad for a first course or light lunch. The spinach leaves, which are sometimes available prewashed and dried, should be young and tender—the smaller the better. If they are large, pull off the stems and tear the leaves into smaller pieces. Watercress leaves can be used in place of the spinach, and a peach vinegar can be substituted for the raspberry.

*T*o make the vinegar-mustard dressing, in a small bowl, combine the vinegar and mustard. Using a whisk or fork, stir until smooth. Add the oil and sugar and whisk or stir until blended. Add salt and pepper to taste and mix well. Set aside.

To make the chutney dressing, in another small bowl, combine the chutney and yogurt. Stir until blended. (If the chutney contains large, irregular pieces of fruit, purée the dressing in a blender or in a food processor fitted with the metal blade, if you wish.) Set aside.

Carefully rinse the spinach, if necessary, and gently spin or pat dry. Place in a large bowl.

Peel, halve and core the pears. Cut each pear half crosswise into thin slices, cutting all the way through but keeping each half intact.

To assemble the salad, drizzle the vinegar-mustard dressing over the spinach leaves and toss to coat the spinach evenly. Divide the spinach among individual plates. Arrange the pear halves, fanning the slices slightly, on top of the spinach. Spoon a generous tablespoon of the chutney dressing over each pear half. Serve at once.

Serves 4

NUTRITIONAL ANALYSIS PER SERVING:

CALORIES 150

(KILOJOULES 630)

PROTEIN 3 G

CARBOHYDRATES 27 G

TOTAL FAT 4 G

SATURATED FAT 0 G

CHOLESTEROL 1 MG

SODIUM 175 MG

DIETARY FIBER 4 G

Chicken Breast Sauté with Vinegar-Tarragon Sauce

1 tablespoon unsalted butter

1 tablespoon vegetable oil

3 tablespoons finely chopped shallots

4 skinless, boneless chicken breast halves, 4–5 oz (125–155 g) each

½ teaspoon salt, plus salt to taste

¼ teaspoon freshly ground pepper, plus pepper to taste

¼ cup (2 fl oz/60 ml) water or low-sodium chicken broth

½ cup (4 fl oz/120 ml) red wine vinegar

2 tablespoons chopped fresh tarragon or 1 teaspoon dried tarragon

1 tablespoon tomato paste

½ teaspoon sugar

2 tablespoons chopped fresh parsley

4 sprigs fresh parsley, optional

*NUTRITIONAL ANALYSIS
PER SERVING:*

CALORIES 197
(KILOJOULES 827)
PROTEIN 27 G
CARBOHYDRATES 4 G
TOTAL FAT 8 G
SATURATED FAT 3 G
CHOLESTEROL 74 MG
SODIUM 382 MG
DIETARY FIBER 0 G

Cooking tempers the bite of vinegar, making it a lively, pleasant sauce for chicken. Classic French recipes for this dish call for lots of butter, but it isn't necessary, as you will see in this version. Serve with mashed potatoes, if you like.

In a large nonstick frying pan over medium heat, melt the butter with the oil. When hot, add the shallots and chicken. Sprinkle with the ½ teaspoon salt and ¼ teaspoon pepper. Cook the chicken, turning once, until browned, 2–3 minutes on each side.

Add the water or broth and ¼ cup (2 fl oz/60 ml) of the vinegar and bring to a boil. Reduce the heat to low, cover and simmer until the chicken is opaque throughout when cut into with a knife, 5–7 minutes. Transfer the chicken to a platter, cover loosely with aluminum foil and keep warm.

Raise the heat to high and add the tarragon and the remaining ¼ cup (2 fl oz/60 ml) vinegar to the pan. Boil rapidly to reduce the liquid by about one-third, about 3 minutes. Remove from the heat, add the tomato paste and sugar and stir or whisk until blended. Season to taste with more salt and pepper, if desired. Pour the sauce over the chicken and sprinkle with the chopped parsley. Serve at once, garnished with parsley sprigs, if desired.

Serves 4

Manicotti with Chicken and Spinach

2½ cups (20 fl oz/625 ml) marinara sauce (*recipe on page 79*)

½ lb (250 g) ground (minced) white chicken or turkey meat

½ cup (2½ oz/75 g) finely chopped yellow onion

1 cup (7 oz/220 g) cooked, drained and chopped spinach

1½ cups (12 oz/375 g) nonfat small-curd cottage cheese

1 teaspoon dried thyme or basil

1 egg

¼ cup (1 oz/30 g) freshly grated Parmesan cheese

½ teaspoon salt

¼ teaspoon freshly ground pepper

8 dried manicotti tubes

NUTRITIONAL ANALYSIS
PER SERVING:

CALORIES 392
(KILOJOULES 1,646)
PROTEIN 35 G
CARBOHYDRATES 41 G
TOTAL FAT 9 G
SATURATED FAT 2 G
CHOLESTEROL 98 MG
SODIUM 1,058 MG
DIETARY FIBER 4 G

Prepare the marinara sauce. Bring a large pot about three-fourths full of water to a rolling boil over high heat.

Meanwhile, coat a nonstick frying pan with nonstick cooking spray and place over medium heat. When hot, add the chicken or turkey and onion and cook, breaking up the meat with a spatula, until the meat is fully cooked, about 10 minutes. Scrape into a large bowl and let cool for 10 minutes.

Put the spinach in a sieve and press against it firmly with the back of a spoon to remove any excess liquid. Add to the chicken along with the cottage cheese, thyme or basil, egg, Parmesan cheese, salt and pepper. Using a wooden spoon, beat vigorously to blend.

Preheat an oven to 325°F (165°C). Spread ½ cup (4 fl oz/ 125 ml) of the sauce over the bottom of an 8-by-12-inch (20-by-30-cm) baking dish or other similarly sized dish.

Add the manicotti tubes to the boiling water, stir well and cook for about 8 minutes; they should remain firm and slightly underdone. Drain them, rinse under cold running water and drain again.

Using a small spoon, stuff each tube with about ⅓ cup (3 oz/ 90 g) of the filling. Arrange in a single layer in the baking dish and spoon the remaining sauce over the top. Cover with aluminum foil and bake until the sauce is bubbling a little around the edges of the dish and the filling is heated through, about 40 minutes.

Remove from the oven and uncover the dish. Let stand for 5 minutes before serving.

Serves 4

Fish Fillets with Black Olive and Caper Relish

½ cup (2½ oz/75 g) chopped black olives
1 tablespoon drained capers
2 tablespoons fresh lemon juice
1 tablespoon olive oil
¼ cup (2 oz/60 g) low-fat plain yogurt
1 tablespoon chopped fresh dill or parsley
¼ teaspoon freshly ground pepper
4 fish fillets, each 6 oz (185 g) and about 1 inch (2.5 cm) thick (*see note*)
lemon wedges
4 fresh dill or parsley sprigs

An uncooked relish perks up mild foods and adds style to any meal. For this quick and simple sauté, use a firm-textured fish such as halibut, snapper or sea bass, or substitute sea scallops for the fish fillets. Accompany with steamed vegetables such as carrots or broccoli.

*I*n a small bowl, combine the olives, capers, lemon juice, oil, yogurt, dill or parsley and pepper. Stir or whisk until well blended. Set aside while you prepare the fish.

Coat a large nonstick frying pan with nonstick cooking spray and place over medium heat. When hot, place the fish fillets in the pan and cook, turning once, until the fillets are well browned and opaque throughout, about 4 minutes on each side.

Transfer the fillets to a warmed platter or individual plates. Spoon the relish evenly over the fish and garnish with lemon wedges and dill or parsley sprigs. Serve at once.

Serves 4

Nutritional Analysis Per Serving:

Calories 251
(Kilojoules 1,054)
Protein 36 g
Carbohydrates 3 g
Total Fat 10 g
Saturated Fat 1 g
Cholesterol 55 mg
Sodium 312 mg
Dietary Fiber 1 g

Beef and Summer Squash Stir-fry

1 lb (500 g) beef flank steak

3 teaspoons cornstarch (cornflour)

2 tablespoons reduced-sodium soy sauce

2 tablespoons dry sherry

½ cup (4 fl oz/120 ml) water

2 zucchini (courgettes)

2 yellow crookneck squashes or 2 more zucchini

1 large yellow onion

4 teaspoons vegetable oil

4 green (spring) onions, including tender green tops, thinly sliced

Steamed rice is a traditional accompaniment to stir-fried meat and vegetables, but mashed potatoes are also a suitable partner.

Trim the flank steak of any visible fat. Cut the steak lengthwise, with the grain, into strips about 2 inches (5 cm) wide. Cut the strips of meat on the diagonal, across the grain, into pieces 2 inches (5 cm) wide and about ¼ inch (6 mm) thick. Place in a large bowl, and sprinkle with 2 teaspoons of the cornstarch; stir and toss until the meat is coated. Set aside.

In a cup, combine the remaining 1 teaspoon cornstarch with the soy sauce, sherry and ¼ cup (2 fl oz/60 ml) of the water; stir until blended, then set aside. Cut the zucchini and crookneck squashes into rounds ¼ inch (6 mm) thick. Thinly slice the yellow onion. Place all of the ingredients next to the stove.

In a nonstick wok or large, deep nonstick frying pan over high heat, warm 2 teaspoons of the oil. When hot but not smoking, add the squashes and yellow onion; toss and stir almost constantly for 3 minutes. Add the remaining ¼ cup (2 fl oz/60 ml) water, cover and cook for 2 minutes. The vegetables should be tender-crisp but not crunchy. Transfer to a shallow dish; set aside. Wipe out the pan with paper towels and return to high heat.

Add the remaining 2 teaspoons oil to the pan. When hot, add the meat and toss and stir constantly for 2 minutes. Return the vegetables and any of their liquid to the pan and stir gently. Whisk the soy sauce mixture briefly to blend it, then add to the pan along with the green onions. Toss and stir until the meat and vegetables are evenly coated and the sauce has thickened slightly, about 1 minute. Serve at once.

Serves 4

Nutritional Analysis
Per Serving:

Calories 323
(Kilojoules 1,357)
Protein 26 g
Carbohydrates 15 g
Total Fat 17 g
Saturated Fat 6 g
Cholesterol 59 mg
Sodium 390 mg
Dietary Fiber 3 g

Chicken Sauté Provençale

2 tablespoons olive oil

4 skinless, boneless chicken breast
halves, 4–5 oz (125–155 g) each

⅓ cup (1½ oz/45 g) finely chopped
yellow onion

2 large cloves garlic, minced

½ teaspoon salt

¼ teaspoon freshly ground pepper

½ cup (4 fl oz/125 ml) dry white wine

1 cup (6 oz/185 g) peeled, seeded and
chopped tomatoes (*see glossary, page
107*)

1 tablespoon chopped fresh marjoram
or oregano or 1 teaspoon dried
marjoram or oregano

1 tablespoon chopped fresh parsley

4 fresh marjoram or parsley sprigs

*This aromatic sauté, quick and simple to prepare, is rich with
the flavors of garlic, wine and tomatoes.*

In a large nonstick frying pan over medium heat, warm
the oil. When hot, add the chicken, onion, garlic, salt and
pepper and cook, turning the chicken once, until lightly
browned, 2–3 minutes on each side. Add the wine and
bring to a boil. Add the tomatoes and chopped marjoram
or oregano and return to a boil. Reduce the heat to low,
cover partially and cook until the sauce has thickened a
little and the chicken is opaque throughout when cut into
with a knife, 5–7 minutes.

Using tongs or a slotted spoon, transfer the chicken to
a warmed platter. Spoon the sauce over the top, sprinkle
with the parsley and garnish with marjoram or parsley
sprigs. Serve at once.

Serves 4

*Nutritional Analysis
Per Serving:*

Calories 222
(Kilojoules 932)
Protein 27 g
Carbohydrates 4 g
Total Fat 8 g
Saturated Fat 1 g
Cholesterol 66 mg
Sodium 354 mg
Dietary Fiber 0 g

41

Spaghetti with Shrimp, Lemon and Snow Peas

2 cups (8 oz/250 g) snow peas
  (mangetouts)
1 lb (500 g) shrimp (prawns), peeled
  and deveined (*see glossary, page 106*)
1 tablespoon cornstarch (cornflour)
1 lb (500 g) dried spaghetti
1 tablespoon olive oil
⅔ cup (5 fl oz/150 ml) low-sodium fish
  stock, bottled clam juice or low-
  sodium chicken broth
¼ cup (2 fl oz/60 ml) fresh lemon juice
2 teaspoons finely grated lemon zest
½ cup (¾ oz/20 g) chopped fresh
  parsley
salt and freshly ground pepper

NUTRITIONAL ANALYSIS
PER SERVING:

CALORIES 590
(KILOJOULES 2,478)
PROTEIN 35 G
CARBOHYDRATES 94 G
TOTAL FAT 7 G
SATURATED FAT 1 G
CHOLESTEROL 140 MG
SODIUM 168 MG
DIETARY FIBER 4 G

When shopping for ingredients to make this recipe, bear in mind one thing: The larger shrimp may look impressive, but the smaller ones generally taste much better and cost much less.

*B*ring a large pot three-fourths full of water to a rolling boil over high heat.

Meanwhile, snap the stem end from each snow pea, pulling it down along the pea to remove any strings; set the peas aside. In a large bowl, toss the shrimp with the cornstarch and set aside.

Add the spaghetti to the boiling water, stir well and cook until *al dente* (tender but firm to the bite), 8–10 minutes, or according to the package directions.

While the spaghetti is cooking, in a large nonstick frying pan over medium-high heat, warm the oil. When hot but not smoking, add the snow peas and the shrimp and stir and toss briskly until the peas are bright green and tender-crisp and the shrimp have started to turn pink, about 2 minutes. Transfer the shrimp and peas to a plate and set aside.

Return the pan to medium-high heat. Add the stock, clam juice or broth, lemon juice and lemon zest and boil for about 1 minute. Return the shrimp and peas to the pan, add the parsley and boil just until the liquid thickens slightly, about 1 minute. Season to taste with salt and pepper.

Drain the spaghetti and place in a warmed shallow serving bowl. Pour the sauce over the spaghetti and toss briefly to combine. Serve at once.

Serves 4

Baked Ratatouille

1 large eggplant (aubergine)

2 zucchini (courgettes)

2 red or green bell peppers (capsicums), or one of each

½ lb (250 g) fresh mushrooms, brushed clean

1 yellow onion

⅓ cup (3 oz/90 g) tomato paste

⅓ cup (3 fl oz/80 ml) red or white wine vinegar

¼ cup (2 fl oz/60 ml) water

2 tablespoons olive oil

2 cloves garlic, minced

1 tablespoon chopped fresh thyme or 1 teaspoon dried thyme

1 teaspoon salt

½ teaspoon freshly ground pepper

½ cup (¾ oz/20 g) chopped fresh basil or parsley

NUTRITIONAL ANALYSIS PER SERVING:

CALORIES 125
(KILOJOULES 525)
PROTEIN 4 G
CARBOHYDRATES 19 G
TOTAL FAT 5 G
SATURATED FAT 0 G
CHOLESTEROL 0 MG
SODIUM 491 MG
DIETARY FIBER 4 G

The communal baking of the vegetables blends their flavors deliciously. Serve ratatouille hot or cold by itself, or with meat or poultry, or hot over pasta. It is also a wonderful spread on crackers or thinly sliced French bread. The ratatouille has many uses, so the recipe makes plenty. It will keep for up to 4 days in the refrigerator.

Preheat an oven to 400°F (200°C). Coat a large roasting pan with nonstick cooking spray.

As you prepare each of the following vegetables, add it to the prepared pan: Cut the unpeeled eggplant into 1-inch (2.5-cm) cubes. Cut the zucchini crosswise into rounds ½ inch (12 mm) thick. Halve the bell peppers through their stem ends and remove the stems, ribs and seeds. Cut the peppers into 1-inch (2.5-cm) squares. Depending upon the size of the mushrooms, cut them into halves or quarters. Thinly slice the onion.

In a small bowl, combine the tomato paste, vinegar, water, oil, garlic, thyme, salt and pepper and stir until blended and smooth. Add to the roasting pan, then stir and toss to combine and coat the vegetables evenly.

Bake until the vegetables begin to soften, about 30 minutes, stirring once at the halfway point. Reduce the heat to 325°F (165°C). Cover the roasting pan and bake until the vegetables are soft and tender but not mushy, about 30 minutes longer, stirring every 10 minutes.

Remove from the oven, uncover and let stand for 10 minutes. Stir in the basil or parsley and serve hot, at room temperature or cold.

Serves 6

Chinese Chicken Salad

1 English (hothouse) cucumber

2 tablespoons vegetable oil

1 tablespoon Asian sesame oil

2 tablespoons reduced-sodium soy sauce

¼ cup (2 fl oz/60 ml) cider vinegar or unseasoned rice wine vinegar

1 tablespoon peeled and grated fresh ginger

2 teaspoons sugar

½ teaspoon red pepper flakes

3 cloves garlic, minced

⅓ cup (1 oz/30 g) thinly sliced green (spring) onions, including tender green tops

⅓ cup (½ oz/15 g) chopped fresh cilantro (fresh coriander), plus sprigs for garnish

2 cups (12 oz/375 g) diced, cooked chicken breast meat

¾ lb (375 g) dried spaghetti or linguine

Don't be daunted by the numerous ingredients, as they go together quickly and their flavors blend to make a wonderful cold chicken salad with Chinese overtones. Serve on a bed of shredded iceberg lettuce, if you wish. This is a good recipe for using leftover cooked chicken breast.

*B*ring a large pot three-fourths full of water to a rolling boil over high heat.

Meanwhile, peel the cucumber, halve it lengthwise and scrape out any seeds. Cut crosswise into slices ¼ inch (6 mm) thick and place in a large bowl. Add the vegetable oil, sesame oil, soy sauce, vinegar, ginger, sugar, pepper flakes, garlic, green onions and cilantro and stir to blend. Add the chicken and toss to coat evenly with the dressing.

Add the pasta to the boiling water, stir well and cook until *al dente* (tender but firm to the bite), about 10 minutes, or according to the package directions. Drain and rinse under cold running water, then drain again.

Add the pasta to the chicken mixture and toss to combine and coat with the dressing. Transfer the salad to a serving bowl or serve on individual plates. Garnish with the cilantro sprigs and refrigerate if not serving within 30 minutes. If refrigerated, bring to room temperature before serving.

Serves 6

NUTRITIONAL ANALYSIS
PER SERVING:

CALORIES 385
(KILOJOULES 1,617)
PROTEIN 26 G
CARBOHYDRATES 47 G
TOTAL FAT 10 G
SATURATED FAT 2 G
CHOLESTEROL 48 MG
SODIUM 250 MG
DIETARY FIBER 2 G

Turkey Breast with Bulgur Stuffing

⅔ cup (5 fl oz/160 ml) boiling water

⅓ cup (2 oz/60 g) bulgur

2 tablespoons olive oil

½ cup (2 oz/60 g) chopped yellow onion

½ cup (2 oz/60 g) chopped celery

1 cup (7 oz/220 g) cooked, drained and chopped spinach

½ cup (1 oz/30 g) fresh white bread crumbs

2 tablespoons chopped fresh sage or 1 teaspoon dried sage

⅓ cup (3 fl oz/80 ml) low-sodium chicken broth or water

1 teaspoon salt, plus salt to taste

½ teaspoon freshly ground pepper, plus pepper to taste

1 skinless, boneless turkey breast half, about 1¾ lb (875 g)

watercress sprigs

NUTRITIONAL ANALYSIS
PER SERVING:

CALORIES 247
(KILOJOULES 1,037)
PROTEIN 35 G
CARBOHYDRATES 12 G
TOTAL FAT 6 G
SATURATED FAT 1 G
CHOLESTEROL 82 MG
SODIUM 495 MG
DIETARY FIBER 3 G

In a small bowl, pour the boiling water over the bulgur, stir and let stand for 1 hour.

Meanwhile, in a large nonstick frying pan over medium-low heat, warm the oil. When hot, add the onion and celery and cook, stirring, until soft, about 5 minutes. Add the spinach and cook, stirring frequently, until the moisture evaporates, about 5 minutes. Transfer to a large bowl and add the bulgur, bread crumbs, sage, broth or water, 1 teaspoon salt and ½ teaspoon pepper. Stir and toss to combine. Set aside.

Preheat an oven to 325°F (165°C). Coat a small roasting pan with nonstick cooking spray.

To butterfly the turkey breast, use a sharp knife to make a horizontal cut along the larger, meatier side of the breast, slicing through to within about ½ inch (12 mm) of the other side; be careful not to cut all the way through. Lift the top piece of meat and fold back to make a large, flat surface. Sprinkle lightly with salt and pepper and spread with the stuffing, mounding it slightly in the center. Bring the pieces of meat together to enclose the stuffing. Using heavy kitchen string, tie the rolled breast in 3 or 4 places around its circumference, then tie around the length to secure both ends and make a cylindrical roll.

Place the turkey in the prepared pan and roast for about 1¼ hours, or until an instant-read thermometer inserted into the center of the roll registers 170°F (77°C). Remove from the oven; cover loosely with aluminum foil and let rest for about 20 minutes before carving.

To serve, snip the strings and discard. Cut the turkey roll crosswise into slices ½ inch (12 mm) thick. Arrange on a platter and garnish with watercress.

Serves 6

Autumn Vegetable Stew

1 small butternut squash, about 1½ lb
(750 g)

4 red boiling potatoes, about 1 lb (500 g)

1 green or red bell pepper (capsicum)

2 tablespoons olive oil

1 large yellow onion, thinly sliced

2 cloves garlic, minced

2 cups (16 fl oz/500 ml) roasted vegetable stock (*recipe on page 11*) or low-
sodium chicken broth

1½ cups (9 oz/280 g) peeled, seeded
and chopped tomatoes (*see glossary,
page 107*)

1½ cups (9 oz/280 g) corn kernels

1 teaspoon dried sage or 1 tablespoon
chopped fresh sage

1 teaspoon salt

¼ teaspoon freshly ground pepper

*NUTRITIONAL ANALYSIS
PER SERVING:*

CALORIES 324
(KILOJOULES 1,361)
PROTEIN 8 G
CARBOHYDRATES 61 G
TOTAL FAT 8 G
SATURATED FAT 1 G
CHOLESTEROL 0 MG
SODIUM 591 MG
DIETARY FIBER 9 G

*This wholesome stew made with a variety of fresh vegetables is
wonderful over brown rice or bulgur, and leftovers are good
cold, drizzled with a few drops of olive oil and vinegar.*

Using a vegetable peeler, peel the squash. Halve it lengthwise, scrape out the seeds and then cut into 1-inch (2.5-cm)
cubes. Cut the unpeeled potatoes into pieces about the
same size. Halve the pepper through the stem end and
remove the stem, ribs and seeds. Cut into 1-inch (2.5-cm)
squares. Set the vegetables aside.

In a large saucepan or a Dutch oven over medium-low
heat, warm the oil. When hot, add the onion and garlic
and cook, stirring occasionally, until the onion has wilted,
about 5 minutes. Add the squash, potatoes, stock or broth,
tomatoes, corn, sage, salt and pepper and stir to combine.
Bring to a boil over medium-high heat, reduce the heat to
low, cover and simmer for 10 minutes to cook the potatoes
and squash partially.

Stir in the bell pepper, raise the heat to medium and
return to a boil. Cover, reduce the heat to low and simmer
until the vegetables are tender but not mushy when
pierced with a knife, 10–15 minutes longer.

Ladle into warmed shallow bowls and serve at once.

Serves 4

Baked Penne with Eggplant, Summer Squash and Tomatoes

6 Asian (slender) eggplants (aubergines)

4 zucchini (courgettes)

2 tablespoons olive oil

1½ cups (9 oz/280 g) peeled and chopped tomatoes (*see glossary, page 107*)

¼ cup (2 oz/60 g) well-drained and chopped oil-packed sun-dried tomatoes

salt and freshly ground pepper

¾ lb (375 g) dried penne

⅓ cup (1½ oz/45 g) freshly grated Parmesan cheese

Here is an ideal pasta dish for a family dinner. Assemble it several hours ahead of time, if you wish, then cover and refrigerate. Just before serving, remove from the refrigerator and bake as directed, increasing the initial baking time by 5 minutes.

*P*reheat an oven to 325°F (165°C). Coat a 3-qt (3-l) baking dish with nonstick cooking spray.

Bring a large pot three-fourths full of water to a rolling boil over high heat.

Meanwhile, cut the eggplants and zucchini crosswise into rounds ½ inch (12 mm) thick. In a large nonstick frying pan over medium-low heat, warm the oil. When hot, add the eggplants and zucchini and cook, stirring occasionally, until softened slightly, about 10 minutes. Add the tomatoes and the sun-dried tomatoes and simmer, uncovered, until the tomatoes are very soft, about 5 minutes. Season to taste with salt and pepper. Remove from the heat and set aside.

Add the penne to the boiling water, stir well and cook until nearly *al dente* (tender but firm to the bite), 10–12 minutes, or according to the package directions. Drain the penne, rinse under cold running water and drain well again.

Transfer the pasta to the prepared baking dish and spoon the vegetable mixture over the top. Stir gently to mix. Sprinkle evenly with the Parmesan cheese.

Cover with aluminum foil and bake for 20 minutes. Uncover and continue to bake until the cheese has melted and browned slightly, about 10 minutes longer. Serve at once.

Serves 4

Nutritional Analysis Per Serving:

Calories 599
(Kilojoules 2,516)
Protein 20 g
Carbohydrates 88 g
Total Fat 20 g
Saturated Fat 4 g
Cholesterol 7 mg
Sodium 203 mg
Dietary Fiber 8 g

Shrimp with Garlicky Tomato Glaze

3 tablespoons olive oil

2 tablespoons tomato paste

¼ cup (2 fl oz/60 ml) red wine vinegar

2 cloves garlic, minced

1 teaspoon dried basil

½ teaspoon red pepper flakes

½ teaspoon salt

1 lb (500 g) large or jumbo shrimp (prawns), peeled and deveined *(see glossary, page 106)*

A spicy tomato marinade becomes a flavorful glaze for these shrimp. Cook them under the broiler or on the grill, and serve over rice.

*I*n a large bowl, combine the olive oil, tomato paste, vinegar, garlic, basil, pepper flakes and salt. Stir until blended and smooth. Add the shrimp and toss to coat evenly. Cover and refrigerate for about 1 hour, tossing occasionally.

Remove the shrimp from the marinade, reserving the marinade.

If you are cooking the shrimp in a broiler (griller), preheat the broiler. Coat the rack of a broiler pan with nonstick cooking spray. Arrange the shrimp on the rack, placing them close together. Broil (grill) about 4 inches (10 cm) from the heat source, turning them once after 3 minutes and brushing with some of the reserved marinade. Continue to broil until the shrimp are pink all over, 2–3 minutes longer.

If you are cooking the shrimp on a grill, prepare a fire in a charcoal grill. Thread the shrimp onto 4 skewers. When the coals are hot, place the skewers on the grill rack 4–6 inches (10–15 cm) above the coals and grill, turning 2 or 3 times and brushing once with some of the reserved marinade after 3 minutes, until the shrimp are pink all over, 6–8 minutes total.

Remove from the broiler or grill and transfer to a warmed platter or individual plates, leaving the shrimp on the skewers, if using. Serve at once.

Serves 4

NUTRITIONAL ANALYSIS
PER SERVING:

CALORIES 200
(KILOJOULES 840)
PROTEIN 19 G
CARBOHYDRATES 4 G
TOTAL FAT 12 G
SATURATED FAT 2 G
CHOLESTEROL 140 MG
SODIUM 475 MG
DIETARY FIBER 0 G

Scallops with Braised Fennel

4 small fennel bulbs, with tops intact

¼ cup (¾ oz/20 g) thinly sliced green (spring) onions, including tender green tops

1¼ lb (625 g) sea scallops

1 tablespoon unsalted butter

2 tablespoons minced shallots

1 cup (8 fl oz/250 ml) roasted vegetable stock (recipe on page 11), low-sodium fish stock or bottled clam juice

½ cup (4 fl oz/125 ml) dry white wine

½ teaspoon salt

¼ teaspoon freshly ground pepper

Cooking the scallops with the braised fennel imbues them with the vegetable's subdued anise flavor. The scallops and fennel, along with the delicate broth, are served in shallow bowls.

Cut off the feathery tops and the stems from the fennel bulbs. Chop enough of the tops to measure about ½ cup (1 oz/30 g). Discard the remaining fennel tops and stems or reserve for another use. In a small bowl, combine ¼ cup (½ oz/15 g) of the chopped fennel tops and the green onions; set aside until serving. Cut away any tough or discolored portions of the fennel bulbs and trim the bulbs. Cut each bulb in half lengthwise; set aside.

If the small, flat muscle, or "foot," attached to the side of each scallop is still intact, cut it off with a sharp knife and discard. Cover and refrigerate the scallops until needed.

In a large nonstick frying pan over medium-low heat, melt the butter. When hot, add the shallots and the remaining ¼ cup (½ oz/15 g) chopped fennel tops and cook gently, stirring, until the shallots wilt slightly and become translucent, about 2 minutes. Add the stock or clam juice, wine, salt and pepper and simmer for 5 minutes to blend the flavors. Add the fennel bulbs, placing them cut side down. Reduce the heat to low, cover and simmer until tender when pierced with a knife, 30–35 minutes.

Add the scallops to the pan, placing them around and between the fennel. Cover and continue to simmer over low heat until the scallops are opaque throughout, 3–4 minutes longer.

Place 2 pieces of fennel in each of 4 shallow bowls. Divide the scallops evenly among the bowls, then ladle the cooking broth over the top. Sprinkle with the fennel–green onion mixture and serve at once.

Serves 4

Nutritional Analysis Per Serving:

Calories 215
(Kilojoules 903)
Protein 27 g
Carbohydrates 12 g
Total Fat 4 g
Saturated Fat 2 g
Cholesterol 55 mg
Sodium 714 mg
Dietary Fiber 2 g

Couscous with Roasted Winter Vegetables

FOR THE VEGETABLES:

½ small butternut squash, ¾ lb (375 g)

2 yellow onions

2 rutabagas (swedes) or turnips, or one of each

2 parsnips

2 carrots

10 or more large cloves garlic

¼ cup (⅓ oz/10 g) chopped fresh sage

3 tablespoons olive oil

1 teaspoon salt

½ teaspoon freshly ground pepper

FOR THE COUSCOUS:

2¼ cups (18 fl oz/560 ml) roasted vegetable stock (recipe on page 11), low-sodium chicken broth or water

1⅓ cups (6½ oz/200 g) quick-cooking couscous

salt and freshly ground pepper

NUTRITIONAL ANALYSIS
PER SERVING:

CALORIES 497

(KILOJOULES 2,087)

PROTEIN 12 G

CARBOHYDRATES 90 G

TOTAL FAT 12 G

SATURATED FAT 2 G

CHOLESTEROL 0 MG

SODIUM 635 MG

DIETARY FIBER 14 G

Oven roasting, an easy cooking method, brings out the full flavor of the vegetables.

Preheat an oven to 425°F (220°C). Coat a large roasting pan with nonstick cooking spray.

As you prepare each of the following vegetables, add it to the pan: Scrape out the seeds from the squash, then, using a vegetable peeler, peel away the skin. Cut the flesh into 1-inch (2.5-cm) cubes. Peel the onions and cut each into 8 wedges. Peel the rutabagas or turnips and cut into 1-inch (2.5-cm) chunks or cubes. Peel the parsnips and carrots, halve them lengthwise and then cut crosswise into 1-inch (2.5-cm) pieces. Add the garlic, sage, oil, salt and pepper to the vegetables. Stir and toss to combine and coat the vegetables evenly.

Bake, stirring occasionally, until the vegetables are lightly browned and tender when pierced with the tip of a sharp knife, 45–55 minutes.

When the vegetables are nearly done, prepare the couscous: Bring the stock, broth or water to a boil in a saucepan. Stir in the couscous, cover and set aside off the heat for 5 minutes. Fluff with a fork and season to taste with salt and pepper.

To serve, mound the couscous on a warmed platter. Spoon the roasted vegetables on top and serve at once.

Serves 4

Open-Faced Steak Sandwiches

2 tablespoons olive oil

2 yellow onions, thinly sliced

½ lb (250 g) fresh mushrooms, brushed clean and thinly sliced

salt and freshly ground pepper

4 beef tenderloin steaks, each 4–5 oz (125-155 g) and ½ inch (12 mm) thick

1 cup (8 fl oz/250 ml) low-sodium beef broth or water

2 English muffins, split and toasted, or 4 crumpets, toasted

4 cups (4 oz/125 g) mixed young, tender salad greens, or tender lettuce leaves, torn in pieces

Because it combines meat, vegetables, salad and bread, this sandwich is truly a complete meal in a single delicious package. Beef tenderloin is boneless and relatively low in fat. It is very tender as long as it is not overcooked.

*I*n a large nonstick frying pan over medium-low heat, warm the oil. When hot, add the onions and mushrooms and stir and toss until softened and wilted a little, about 3 minutes. Season to taste with salt and pepper. Transfer the vegetables to a bowl and cover to keep warm.

Raise the heat to high and return the pan to the stove. Add the steaks to the hot pan and cook, turning once, until well browned and done to your liking, 2–3 minutes on each side for medium-rare. Season to taste with salt and pepper. Transfer the steaks to a plate and set aside. Add the broth or water and boil rapidly for a minute or two, stirring to scrape up any browned bits from the pan bottom. Remove from the heat.

To serve, place a toasted muffin half or crumpet on each plate. Top each with one-fourth of the salad greens and one-fourth of the onion-mushroom mixture. Put a steak on top of the mushroom-onion mixture and spoon some pan juices over the steak. Serve at once.

Serves 4

NUTRITIONAL ANALYSIS
PER SERVING:

CALORIES 504
(KILOJOULES 2,117)
PROTEIN 26 G
CARBOHYDRATES 24 G
TOTAL FAT 34 G
SATURATED FAT 12 G
CHOLESTEROL 81 MG
SODIUM 212 MG
DIETARY FIBER 3 G

Risotto Primavera

1 yellow onion
6 fresh mushrooms, brushed clean
1 green or red bell pepper (capsicum)
1 yellow zucchini (courgette) or
   crookneck squash
½ lb (250 g) asparagus
3–3½ cups (24–28 fl oz/750–875 ml)
   roasted vegetable stock (recipe on
   page 11) or low-sodium chicken broth
2 tablespoons olive oil
1¼ cups (9 oz/280 g) Arborio rice or
   other medium-grained white rice
½ cup (4 fl oz/125 ml) dry white wine
½ cup (2 oz/60 g) freshly grated
   Parmesan cheese
salt and freshly ground pepper

*Nutritional Analysis
Per Serving:*

Calories 421
(Kilojoules 1,768)
Protein 12 g
Carbohydrates 63 g
Total Fat 11 g
Saturated Fat 3 g
Cholesterol 10 mg
Sodium 249 mg
Dietary Fiber 3 g

*T*hinly slice the onion and the mushrooms. Halve the bell pepper through the stem end; remove the stem, ribs and seeds. Cut into long strips about ¼ inch (6 mm) wide. Quarter the zucchini or crookneck squash lengthwise; cut crosswise into pieces ¼ inch (6 mm) thick. Cut off the top 2 inches (5 cm) from each asparagus spear (save the bottoms for another use); cut on the diagonal into pieces ½ inch (12 mm) thick. Set the vegetables aside separately.

Pour the stock or broth into a saucepan and bring to a simmer. Adjust the heat to maintain a gentle simmer.

Meanwhile, in a large saucepan or deep nonstick frying pan over medium-low heat, warm the olive oil. When hot, add the onion and mushrooms and sauté, stirring, until softened, about 3 minutes. Add the rice and stir until the kernels are coated with the oil, about 2 minutes more. Add the wine and cook, stirring frequently, until most of it has been absorbed, about 3 minutes.

Reduce the heat to low and add the bell pepper and 1 cup (8 fl oz/250 ml) of the hot stock or broth. Cook, stirring frequently, until most of it has been absorbed, about 5 minutes.

Add the squash and asparagus and another 1 cup (8 fl oz/ 250 ml) of the hot stock or broth and simmer, stirring often, until most of it has been absorbed. Add another 1 cup (8 fl oz/ 250 ml) of the hot stock or broth and simmer, stirring occasionally, until it is has been absorbed and the risotto has a creamy consistency. Taste the rice; if it is hard in the center, add the remaining ½ cup (4 fl oz/125 ml) stock or broth and simmer, stirring, until absorbed and the grains are tender but slightly *al dente* (firm to the bite). Total cooking time is about 25 minutes.

Stir in the Parmesan cheese and season to taste with salt and pepper. Serve at once.

Serves 4

Pork Tenderloin with Chutney Dressing

2 tablespoons vegetable oil

2 teaspoons dried thyme or sage

½ teaspoon salt

½ teaspoon freshly ground pepper

2 pork tenderloins, about ¾ lb (375 g)
   each

½ cup (5 oz/155 g) mango chutney

½ cup (4½ oz/140 g) applesauce

¼ cup (2 fl oz/60 ml) tomato catsup

1½ teaspoons curry powder

The unusual blend of ingredients in the dressing complements the naturally rich flavor of the pork. This is good served hot or cold. If serving cold, let the tenderloins cool before slicing, then arrange over a bed of romaine (cos) or butter (Boston) lettuce.

Preheat an oven to 350°F (180°C).

   In a small cup, stir together the oil, thyme or sage, salt and pepper. Trim the pork tenderloins of any visible fat. Rub the herb mixture evenly over the pork. Place the tenderloins in a roasting pan and roast until firm to the touch and pale pink when cut in the thickest portion, about 40 minutes. To test for doneness, insert an instant-read thermometer into the thickest part of a tenderloin; it should read 160°F (71°C). Remove from the oven and set aside for 5 minutes before slicing.

   Meanwhile, in a small bowl, stir together the chutney, applesauce, catsup and curry powder until well blended.

   To serve, cut the pork on the diagonal into slices ¼–½ inch (6–12 mm) thick. Arrange the slices, overlapping slightly, on a platter. Serve at once and pass the dressing at the table.

Serves 6

*Nutritional Analysis
Per Serving:*

Calories 258
(Kilojoules 1,084)
Protein 24 g
Carbohydrates 20 g
Total Fat 9 g
Saturated Fat 2 g
Cholesterol 66 mg
Sodium 557 mg
Dietary Fiber 1 g

Fettuccine with Sausage, Garlic and Mushrooms

¾ lb (375 g) cooked low-fat smoked chicken or turkey sausages
1 tablespoon olive oil
2 large cloves garlic, minced
1 lb (500 g) fresh mushrooms, brushed clean and thinly sliced
1 cup (8 fl oz/250 ml) dry white wine
¼ cup (⅓ oz/10 g) chopped fresh parsley
salt and freshly ground pepper
1 lb (500 g) dried fettuccine

Mushrooms, garlic and sausage give this fettuccine in wine-flavored broth an alluring blend of textures and flavors. Omit the sausage for a vegetarian meal.

*B*ring a large pot three-fourths full of water to a rolling boil over high heat.

Slice the sausage into rounds about ¼ inch (6 mm) thick. In a large nonstick frying pan over medium heat, warm the oil. When hot, add the sausage slices and cook, stirring occasionally, until lightly browned, 3–4 minutes. Add the garlic and mushrooms and stir until the mushrooms have softened and released some of their liquid, about 3 minutes. Add the wine and boil over medium heat until the mushrooms are tender, about 3 minutes longer. Stir in the parsley and season to taste with salt and pepper.

While the sauce is cooking, add the fettuccine to the boiling water, stir well and cook until *al dente* (tender but firm to the bite), 8–10 minutes, or according to the package directions.

Drain the fettuccine and place in a warmed shallow serving bowl. Pour the sauce over the top and toss briefly to combine. Serve at once.

Serves 6

Nutritional Analysis Per Serving:

Calories 437
(Kilojoules 1,835)
Protein 21 g
Carbohydrates 60 g
Total Fat 10 g
Saturated Fat 4 g
Cholesterol 102 mg
Sodium 813 mg
Dietary Fiber 3 g

Salmon Fillets with Chive Sauce

FOR THE CHIVE SAUCE:

½ cup (¾ oz/20 g) finely chopped fresh
    chives
⅓ cup (2½ oz/75 g) low-fat plain yogurt
2 tablespoons finely chopped dill pickle
    or sweet pickle
2 tablespoons low-fat mayonnaise
2 tablespoons fresh lemon juice
2 teaspoons chopped drained capers
½ teaspoon sugar
¼ teaspoon salt
pinch of freshly ground pepper

FOR THE SALMON:

2 tablespoons chopped fresh dill or
    2 teaspoons dried dill
2 teaspoons finely grated lemon zest
2 teaspoons paprika
½ teaspoon salt
¼ teaspoon cayenne pepper
4 skinless salmon fillets, each 6 oz (185 g)
    and about 1 inch (2.5 cm) thick
2 teaspoons olive oil
fresh dill sprigs and lemon slices

NUTRITIONAL ANALYSIS
PER SERVING:

CALORIES 299
(KILOJOULES 1,256)
PROTEIN 35 G
CARBOHYDRATES 6 G
TOTAL FAT 14 G
SATURATED FAT 2 G
CHOLESTEROL 95 MG
SODIUM 666 MG
DIETARY FIBER 0 G

The chive sauce will complement nearly any fish. It will remind you of tartar sauce, although it is lower in calories. A little sugar softens the tang of the yogurt.

To make the chive sauce, in a small bowl, combine the chives, yogurt, pickle, mayonnaise, lemon juice, capers, sugar, salt and pepper. Using a whisk or fork, stir together until well blended. Cover and refrigerate; bring to room temperature before serving.

To prepare the salmon, in a small bowl, combine the dill, lemon zest, paprika, salt and cayenne. Rub each fish fillet with ½ teaspoon of the oil, then rub with the dill mixture, coating the fillets evenly. Transfer to a plate, cover and refrigerate for 1–2 hours.

Coat a large nonstick frying pan with nonstick cooking spray and place over medium-high heat. When hot but not smoking, place the salmon fillets in the pan and cook, turning once, until the fillets are well browned and opaque throughout, 3–4 minutes on each side.

To serve, transfer the fillets to a warmed platter or individual plates. Garnish with dill sprigs and lemon slices and accompany with the chive sauce.

Serves 4

Smothered Chicken with Mushrooms and Onions

1 large carrot

1 large yellow onion, thinly sliced

¾ lb (375 g) fresh mushrooms, brushed clean and thinly sliced

4 skinless, boneless chicken breast halves, 4–5 oz (125–155 g) each

½ teaspoon salt, plus salt to taste

¼ teaspoon freshly ground pepper, plus pepper to taste

2 tablespoons vegetable oil

¼ cup (1½ oz/45 g) all-purpose (plain) flour

2 cups (16 fl oz/500 ml) low-sodium chicken broth

2 tablespoons chopped fresh tarragon or ½ teaspoon dried tarragon

Nutritional Analysis Per Serving:

Calories 292

(Kilojoules 1,226)

Protein 32 g

Carbohydrates 20 g

Total Fat 10 g

Saturated Fat 2 g

Cholesterol 66 mg

Sodium 419 mg

Dietary Fiber 3 g

Smothered chicken is an old-fashioned dish that commonly appeared in early cookbooks. It is satisfying, filling and full of flavor, and is delicious served over rice.

*P*eel the carrot, quarter it lengthwise and then cut cross-wise into pieces ½ inch (12 mm) thick. Set aside with the onion and mushrooms.

Coat a large nonstick frying pan with nonstick cooking spray and place over medium-high heat. When hot but not smoking, add the chicken breast halves and sprinkle with the ½ teaspoon salt and ¼ teaspoon pepper. Cook, turning once, until browned, about 2 minutes on each side. Transfer the chicken to a plate and set aside.

Return the pan to medium-high heat and add the oil. When hot but not smoking, add the carrot, onion and mushrooms and cook briskly, stirring frequently, until the vegetables have softened and are lightly browned, about 7 minutes. Sprinkle with the flour and cook, stirring constantly, until fully blended, about 2 minutes longer. Add the broth and tarragon and bring to a boil, stirring frequently until slightly thickened. Return the chicken breasts to the pan, pushing them down into the liquid. Reduce the heat to low, cover and simmer until the chicken breasts are opaque throughout when cut into with a knife and the vegetables are tender, about 10 minutes.

Season to taste with salt and pepper and serve at once.

Serves 4

Baked Fish with Braised Endive

8 heads Belgian endive (chicory/witloof)
1 tablespoon unsalted butter
1 tablespoon olive oil
1½ cups (12 fl oz/375 ml) roasted
   vegetable stock (recipe on page 11),
   bottled clam juice or low-sodium
   chicken broth, or as needed
1 tablespoon fresh lemon juice
4 firm-textured fish fillets, each 6 oz
   (185 g) and about 1 inch (2.5 cm)
   thick (see note)
salt and freshly ground pepper

Braising transforms raw endive from crisp and slightly bitter to tender and subtle—a perfect companion to fish. Almost any firm-textured fish will work here. Try halibut, sea bass or salmon.

Rinse the endives, pat dry with paper towels and trim off any browned leaves or spots; set aside.

Preheat an oven to 325°F (165°C). For cooking the fish and endives, you will need a large frying pan (not cast iron) or a flameproof baking dish—something that can go from the stove top to the oven.

In the frying pan or baking dish over medium heat, melt the butter with the oil. When hot, add the endives and cook, turning frequently, until browned in spots, about 5 minutes. (Be careful, as the hot oil can pop; a spatter shield is useful.) Add the stock, clam juice or broth and the lemon juice. The liquid should be at a depth of ⅓–½ inch (9–12 mm); add more if necessary. Bring to a boil over medium heat, cover and place in the oven. Bake until the endives are a pale cream color and the heads have shrunk and wilted slightly, 35–40 minutes.

Remove from the oven and lay the fish fillets in a single layer among the endives. Cover and return to the oven until the fillets are opaque throughout, 10–12 minutes.

Transfer the fish and endives to a warmed platter and cover loosely with aluminum foil to keep warm. Place the pan or dish over high heat and boil the cooking liquid rapidly until it is reduced to about ½ cup (4 fl oz/125 ml).

Season the liquid to taste with salt and pepper and pour over the fish. Serve at once.

Serves 4

NUTRITIONAL ANALYSIS
PER SERVING:

CALORIES 267
(KILOJOULES 1,121)
PROTEIN 37 G
CARBOHYDRATES 5 G
TOTAL FAT 10 G
SATURATED FAT 3 G
CHOLESTEROL 62 MG
SODIUM 106 MG
DIETARY FIBER 3 G

California Fish Stew

½ lb (250 g) sea scallops

½ lb (250 g) large shrimp (prawns),
   peeled and deveined (see glossary,
   page 106)

1 lb (500 g) skinless fish fillets such
   as cod or snapper

2 tablespoons olive oil

3 cloves garlic, minced

1 cup (8 fl oz/250 ml) dry white wine

⅓ cup (3 fl oz/80 ml) water

2 cups (12 oz/375 g) peeled, seeded
   and chopped tomatoes (see glossary,
   page 107)

1 teaspoon dried oregano or thyme

½ teaspoon salt

¼ teaspoon freshly ground pepper

⅓ cup (½ oz/15 g) chopped fresh
   parsley, preferably flat-leaf (Italian)

NUTRITIONAL ANALYSIS
PER SERVING:

CALORIES 316
(KILOJOULES 1,327)
PROTEIN 40 G
CARBOHYDRATES 7 G
TOTAL FAT 9 G
SATURATED FAT 1 G
CHOLESTEROL 138 MG
SODIUM 507 MG
DIETARY FIBER 1 G

Have the ingredients prepared and near the stove, because this fish stew cooks in just minutes. The fish and shellfish are added in two batches, which results in a more flavorful dish. With it you need only a green salad and good bread, and a light, refreshing dessert such as lemon ice with berry sauce (recipe on page 97). Just about any firm, white-fleshed fish can be used.

*I*f the small, flat muscle, or "foot," attached to the side of each scallop is still intact, cut it off with a sharp knife and discard.

Cut all the fish and shellfish into ¾–1-inch (2–2.5-cm) pieces. Check for any errant bones and discard. Place in a large bowl and set aside.

In a large saucepan or deep nonstick frying pan over medium-low heat, warm the oil. When hot, add the garlic and sauté, stirring, for about 30 seconds. Add half of the fish and shellfish and then all of the wine, water, tomatoes, oregano or thyme, salt and pepper. Raise the heat to high and bring to a gentle boil; lower the heat and boil gently for 1 minute. Stir, reduce the heat to low, cover and cook for 2 minutes longer.

Add the remaining fish and shellfish and cook, stirring gently, just until all the pieces are opaque throughout, about 3 minutes. Stir in the parsley and serve at once.

Serves 4

Pork Tenderloin with Braised Cabbage

1 large head green cabbage
2 pork tenderloins, about ¾ lb (375 g)
 each
1 tablespoon vegetable oil
salt to taste, plus 1 teaspoon salt
freshly ground pepper to taste, plus
 ¼ teaspoon pepper
2 tablespoons cider vinegar
1 tablespoon sugar

Lean and boneless, pork tenderloins cook quickly, so they're easy to "pan-roast" with cabbage on the stove top. This dish needs only mashed or boiled potatoes to round out the menu.

Remove any bruised outer leaves from the cabbage and discard. Cut the head of cabbage into quarters through the stem end and then remove the central core from each wedge. Slice the wedges crosswise into thin shreds. You should have about 10 cups (30 oz/940 g) shredded cabbage. Set aside.

Trim the pork tenderloins of any visible fat. In a large nonstick frying pan over medium-high heat, warm the oil. When hot but not smoking, add the tenderloins, season lightly with salt and pepper, and cook, turning frequently, until browned on all sides, about 10 minutes. Remove from the pan and set aside.

Return the pan to medium-high heat. Add the cabbage, the 1 teaspoon salt and the ¼ teaspoon pepper and cook, stirring and tossing several times, until the cabbage is slightly wilted, about 5 minutes. Add the vinegar and sprinkle on the sugar; stir and toss to combine. Reduce the heat to low and return the pork to the pan, pressing the tenderloins down slightly into the cabbage. Cover and cook until the cabbage is tender and the pork is firm to the touch and pale pink when cut in the thickest portion, about 20 minutes. To test for doneness, insert an instant-read thermometer into the thickest part of a tenderloin; it should read 160°F (71°C).

Transfer the tenderloins to a cutting board. Mound the cabbage on a platter. Cut the tenderloins on the diagonal into thin slices and arrange over the cabbage. Serve at once.

Serves 6

NUTRITIONAL ANALYSIS
PER SERVING:

CALORIES 199
(KILOJOULES 836)
PROTEIN 26 G
CARBOHYDRATES 10 G
TOTAL FAT 6 G
SATURATED FAT 2 G
CHOLESTEROL 74 MG
SODIUM 449 MG
DIETARY FIBER 3 G

Spaghetti with Marinara Sauce

FOR THE SAUCE:

2 tablespoons olive oil

1 yellow onion, chopped

2 cloves garlic, minced

¼ lb (125 g) fresh mushrooms, brushed clean and sliced

1 can (28 oz/875 g) crushed tomatoes in purée

⅓ cup (3 fl oz/80 ml) dry red or white wine or water

¼ cup (2 oz/60 g) tomato paste

½ teaspoon dried thyme or oregano or mixed Italian herbs

salt and freshly ground pepper

FOR THE SPAGHETTI:

1 lb (500 g) dried spaghetti

1 cup (4 oz/125 g) freshly grated Parmesan cheese

NUTRITIONAL ANALYSIS PER SERVING:

CALORIES 465

(KILOJOULES 1,953)

PROTEIN 19 G

CARBOHYDRATES 71 G

TOTAL FAT 11 G

SATURATED FAT 4 G

CHOLESTEROL 13 MG

SODIUM 607 MG

DIETARY FIBER 4 G

Quick to make, this basic Italian-style tomato sauce is handy to have on hand, as it complements a wide variety of pastas, from spaghetti and linguine to rigatoni or other tube shapes. The recipe yields about 4 cups (32 fl oz/1 l) sauce, enough for 1 pound (500 g) of pasta. It will keep several days in the refrigerator or several months in the freezer. This same sauce is used for the manicotti with chicken and spinach on page 34.

Bring a large pot three-fourths full of water to a rolling boil over high heat.

To make the sauce, in a saucepan over medium-low heat, warm the olive oil. When hot, add the onion, garlic and mushrooms and cook, stirring frequently, until the vegetables are soft, about 7 minutes.

Add the tomatoes, wine or water, tomato paste and herb(s) and stir to combine. Bring to a boil over medium-high heat, then return the heat to medium-low and simmer uncovered, stirring occasionally, until the sauce thickens slightly, 10–15 minutes. Season to taste with salt and pepper.

While the sauce is simmering, add the spaghetti to the boiling water, stir well and cook until *al dente* (tender but firm to the bite), about 10 minutes, or according to the package directions.

Drain the spaghetti and place in a warmed shallow serving bowl. Pour the sauce over the top and toss briefly to combine. Serve at once. Pass the Parmesan cheese at the table.

Serves 6

Polenta with Pesto

FOR THE POLENTA:

1½ cups (12 fl oz/375 ml) water

1½ cups (12 fl oz/375 ml) nonfat milk

1 tablespoon unsalted butter

1 teaspoon salt

pinch of red pepper flakes

¾ cup (4 oz/125 g) polenta or yellow
cornmeal

FOR THE PESTO:

3 cups (3 oz/90 g) loosely packed fresh
basil leaves

½ cup (½ oz/15 g) fresh flat-leaf (Italian)
parsley sprigs or 1 cup (1 oz/30 g)
fresh curly-leaf parsley sprigs

2 large cloves garlic

¼ cup (2 fl oz/60 ml) olive oil

½ teaspoon salt

¼ cup (1 oz/30 g) freshly grated
Parmesan cheese

NUTRITIONAL ANALYSIS
PER SERVING:

CALORIES 348
(KILOJOULES 1,462)
PROTEIN 10 G
CARBOHYDRATES 36 G
TOTAL FAT 20 G
SATURATED FAT 5 G
CHOLESTEROL 14 MG
SODIUM 992 MG
DIETARY FIBER 2 G

With its robust texture, polenta has a natural affinity for a variety of toppings and sauces. Sliced and browned, it makes a delicious base for pesto or tomato sauce, or for grilled chicken or fish.

Coat a 9-inch (23-cm) round pie pan with nonstick cooking spray.

To make the polenta, in a saucepan, combine the water, milk, butter, salt and pepper flakes and bring to a boil over high heat. Slowly pour in the polenta or cornmeal, whisking constantly so that it does not lump. Reduce the heat to low and cook, stirring frequently, until quite thick, 10–15 minutes; it should have the consistency of cooked oatmeal. Spread evenly in the pie pan, then cover with plastic wrap and chill until firm, about 1½ hours.

Meanwhile, make the pesto: In a food processor fitted with the metal blade, place the basil, parsley and garlic. Process until puréed. With the motor running, add the olive oil in a thin, steady stream. Add the salt and cheese and process until smooth. If the pesto seems too thick, add 1–2 tablespoons water. You should have at least ¾ cup (6 fl oz/180 ml). Set aside. (At this point, the pesto can be refrigerated in a tightly covered container for up to 3 days, or frozen for several months.)

Cut the polenta into 8 wedges and remove from the pie pan with a spatula. Coat a large nonstick frying pan with nonstick cooking spray and place over medium-high heat. When hot, add the polenta wedges and cook, turning once, until lightly browned, about 3 minutes on each side.

To serve, transfer the wedges to a warmed platter or individual plates. Spoon half of the pesto over the wedges. Pass the remaining pesto at the table.

Serves 4

Citrus-Marinated Cornish Hens

4 Cornish game hens, 1½ lb (750 g) each

2 teaspoons finely grated lemon zest

½ cup (4 fl oz/125 ml) fresh lemon or lime juice

½ cup (4 fl oz/125 ml) fresh orange juice

2 cloves garlic, minced

2 tablespoons minced shallots or green (spring) onions

½ teaspoon salt

½ fresh jalapeño chili pepper, seeded and minced

10 fresh thyme or rosemary sprigs, plus sprigs for garnish

lemon, lime and/or orange slices

Nutritional Analysis Per Serving:

Calories 754
(Kilojoules 3,167)
Protein 83 g
Carbohydrates 9 g
Total Fat 41 g
Saturated Fat 11 g
Cholesterol 264 mg
Sodium 522 mg
Dietary Fiber 0 g

*F*irst, butterfly the game hens: Place each hen, breast side down, on a work surface. With heavy-duty kitchen scissors, cut from the neck to the tail along both sides of the backbone; lift out the backbone. Turn breast side up and, using the heel of your hand, press down firmly on the breastbone to flatten it. Cut off the tips of the wings and discard. Put the hens in a heavy-duty, lock-top plastic bag; set aside.

In a small bowl, stir together the lemon zest, lemon or lime juice, orange juice, garlic, shallots or green onions, salt and jalapeño pepper. Pour into the plastic bag with the hens. Press out the air from the bag and seal closed. Set in a bowl and marinate in the refrigerator for at least 2 hours or as long as overnight.

Preheat an oven to 425°F (220°C). Coat a large roasting pan with nonstick cooking spray.

Remove the hens from the marinade and pat them dry with paper towels. Reserve the marinade. Place 5 of the thyme or rosemary sprigs in the prepared pan and put the hens, breast side up, on top in a single layer, laying them flat. Tuck the remaining 5 herb sprigs around the hens.

Roast for 15 minutes. Brush with some of the reserved marinade, then reduce the heat to 325°F (165°C). Roast for 15 minutes and brush again with the reserved marinade. Continue roasting until the skin is well browned and the meat is no longer pink when cut at the bone, about 15 minutes longer. Alternatively, test for doneness with an instant-read thermometer: Insert into the thickest part of the breast or thigh away from the bone; it should read 170°F (77°C) in the breast and 185°F (85°C) in the thigh. Total cooking time is about 45 minutes.

Transfer the hens to a platter or individual plates and spoon the pan juices over the top. Garnish with herb sprigs and lemon, lime and/or orange slices. Serve at once.

Serves 4

Ginger Baked Apples

4 large apples (*see note*)

⅓ cup (2½ oz/75 g) firmly packed
  brown sugar

⅓ cup (2 oz/60 g) dried currants or
  raisins

3 tablespoons finely chopped candied
  ginger

¼ teaspoon ground cinnamon

pinch of salt

1 tablespoon unsalted butter, at room
  temperature

⅓ cup (3 fl oz/80 ml) water

1 tablespoon granulated sugar

Baked apples are soothing fare, and they are equally suitable for breakfast or dessert. The best apples for baking vary according to where you live. Reliable, widely available varieties include Golden Delicious and Rome Beauty.

Preheat an oven to 325°F (165°C).

Using a vegetable peeler, and working from the blossom end—not the larger stem end—peel the apples about half-way down. Using an apple corer or paring knife, core them. Then use the point of a knife to dislodge any stubborn seeds from the center hole. Place the apples, larger ends down, in a baking dish just large enough to hold them comfortably.

In a small bowl, combine the brown sugar, currants or raisins, ginger, cinnamon, salt and butter. Using your fingertips or the back of a spoon, mash the ingredients together until blended into a damp, crumbly paste. Pack about 2 tablespoons of the mixture in the center of each apple, pressing it in with your fingers. Pour the water into the dish.

Cover the dish snugly with aluminum foil and bake for about 40 minutes. Remove from the oven and sprinkle the apples evenly with the granulated sugar. Return to the oven and bake, uncovered, until the apples are just tender when pierced with the tip of a sharp knife, about 10 minutes. Don't overbake or the apples will become mushy.

Using a spatula, transfer the apples to individual dessert plates or a platter, then spoon the pan juices over them. Serve warm.

Serves 4

NUTRITIONAL ANALYSIS
PER SERVING:

CALORIES 287
(KILOJOULES 1,205)
PROTEIN 1 G
CARBOHYDRATES 68 G
TOTAL FAT 4 G
SATURATED FAT 2 G
CHOLESTEROL 8 MG
SODIUM 49 MG
DIETARY FIBER 5 G

Caramel Baked Bananas

2 tablespoons unsalted butter, cut into pieces

1 tablespoon fresh lemon juice

½ teaspoon vanilla extract (essence)

¼ teaspoon ground cinnamon

pinch of salt

½ cup (3½ oz/100 g) firmly packed brown sugar

4 firm, ripe bananas

2 tablespoons low-fat evaporated milk

Baked bananas have an appealing, creamy taste and texture. And there is no better accompaniment than caramel sauce, which practically makes itself during the baking.

*P*reheat an oven to 350°F (180°C).

In an 8-inch (20-cm) square cake pan or a 9-inch (23-cm) round pie pan, combine the butter, lemon juice, vanilla, cinnamon, salt and ¼ cup (1¾ oz/50 g) of the brown sugar. Place in the oven until the butter melts, about 3 minutes. Remove from the oven and stir with a fork to blend.

Peel the bananas, put them in the baking pan and turn them to coat evenly with the butter mixture. Sprinkle the bananas with the remaining ¼ cup (1¾ oz/50 g) brown sugar. Bake, uncovered, until the sauce is bubbling and the bananas are barely tender when pierced, about 15 minutes.

Using a spatula, carefully transfer the bananas to a platter or individual plates. Add the evaporated milk to the baking pan and stir briskly with a fork or whisk until creamy and smooth. Pour the sauce over the bananas. Serve at once.

Serves 4

Nutritional Analysis Per Serving:

Calories 259
(Kilojoules 1,088)
Protein 2 g
Carbohydrates 52 g
Total Fat 6 g
Saturated Fat 4 g
Cholesterol 17 mg
Sodium 53 mg
Dietary Fiber 2 g

Summer Fruit Parfaits

1½ teaspoons unflavored gelatin
¼ cup (2 fl oz/60 ml) nonfat milk
1 cup (8 oz/250 g) low-fat cottage cheese
⅓ cup (3 oz/90 g) low-fat plain yogurt
1½ teaspoons vanilla extract (essence)
pinch of salt
8 tablespoons (4 oz/125 g) sugar
3 ripe freestone peaches
2 cups (8 oz/250 g) berries such as
   raspberries, blueberries or sliced
   strawberries, or a mixture
2 tablespoons rum or orange liqueur
2 tablespoons finely crushed
   gingersnaps, optional

A purée of cottage cheese and yogurt, sweetened and flavored, makes a luxurious, low-fat substitute for the ice cream and whipped cream used in traditional parfaits.

*I*n a small saucepan, sprinkle the gelatin over the milk, stir and let stand for several minutes to soften.

   In a food processor fitted with the metal blade or in a blender, combine the cottage cheese, yogurt, vanilla, salt and 6 table-spoons (3 oz/90 g) of the sugar. Process until smooth. Scrape the mixture into a bowl.

   Place the saucepan with the softened gelatin over low heat and stir until the gelatin granules have dissolved, about 2 minutes. Watch carefully and do not allow to boil. Add the gelatin to the cheese mixture and whisk to mix thoroughly. Cover and refrigerate, stirring occasionally, until chilled, 1–2 hours; the mixture should remain quite soft.

   Bring a saucepan three-fourths full of water to a boil. Immerse the peaches in the water for 30 seconds, then, using a slotted spoon, transfer to a work surface. When cool enough to handle, slip off the skins. Halve and pit the peaches, then slice.

   In a bowl, combine the peaches, berries, rum or orange liqueur and remaining 2 tablespoons sugar. Toss to mix.

   To assemble the parfaits, in 4 glass dishes, alternate layers of the cheese and fruit mixtures, beginning with the cheese and ending with the fruit. Or layer the cheese and fruit mixtures in a large glass bowl. Dust the top(s) with the gingersnap crumbs, if using, and refrigerate for up to 6 hours before serving.

Serves 4

Nutritional Analysis Per Serving:

Calories 268
(Kilojoules 1,126)
Protein 11 g
Carbohydrates 52 g
Total Fat 1 g
Saturated Fat 0 g
Cholesterol 7 mg
Sodium 259 mg
Dietary Fiber 4 g

Gingerbread with Poached Pears

FOR THE POACHED PEARS:

2 cups (16 fl oz/500 ml) dry red or
white wine
½ cup (4 oz/125 g) sugar
1 cinnamon stick, 3 inches (7.5 cm) long
1 tablespoon finely grated orange zest,
plus thin zest strips for garnish
4 firm, ripe pears, preferably Bosc,
peeled, halved and cored

FOR THE GINGERBREAD:

⅓ cup (2 oz/60 g) thinly sliced, unpeeled
fresh ginger
¾ cup (6 oz/185 g) firmly packed light
brown sugar
2 tablespoons molasses
¼ cup (2 fl oz/60 ml) vegetable oil
1 egg
¾ cup (6 oz/185 g) nonfat plain yogurt
1½ cups (6 oz/185 g) cake (soft-wheat)
flour
½ teaspoon salt
1 teaspoon baking soda (bicarbonate
of soda)
1 teaspoon ground cinnamon

NUTRITIONAL ANALYSIS
PER SERVING:

CALORIES 367
(KILOJOULES 1,541)
PROTEIN 4 G
CARBOHYDRATES 72 G
TOTAL FAT 8 G
SATURATED FAT 1 G
CHOLESTEROL 27 MG
SODIUM 333 MG
DIETARY FIBER 2 G

*T*o poach the pears, in a saucepan, combine the wine, sugar, cinnamon stick and grated orange zest. Bring to a boil over high heat, stirring to dissolve the sugar. Reduce the heat to low and simmer, uncovered, for 5 minutes. Place the pear halves in the liquid, adding water if needed to cover them completely. Cover and simmer gently until tender but still firm when pierced with the tip of a sharp knife, about 20 minutes. Remove from the heat and let the pears cool in the liquid for at least 2 hours before serving. (The poached pears will keep, covered and refrigerated, for several days. Bring to room temperature before serving.)

Preheat an oven to 350°F (180°C). Coat an 8-inch (20-cm) square cake pan with nonstick cooking spray.

To make the gingerbread, in a food processor fitted with the metal blade, finely chop the ginger. Scrape into a small saucepan and add ¼ cup (2 oz/60 g) of the brown sugar. Cook over medium heat, stirring constantly, until the sugar has melted and the ginger is very aromatic, about 2 minutes. Stir in the molasses and set aside.

In a bowl, combine the oil, egg, yogurt and remaining ½ cup (4 oz/125 g) brown sugar. Using a wire whisk or a fork, beat until blended. In a bowl, combine the cake flour, salt, baking soda and cinnamon and sift directly onto the yogurt mixture. Add the ginger mixture and beat just until the batter is blended. Pour into the prepared pan.

Bake until a toothpick inserted into the center comes out clean, 25–30 minutes. Remove from the oven and let cool in the pan.

Cut the gingerbread into squares and serve on individual plates. Accompany each piece with a poached pear half and garnish with a strip of orange zest.

Serves 8

Zesty Fruit Sherbet

1 lb (500 g) peaches or strawberries
⅔ cup (5 oz/155 g) sugar
¼ cup (2½ oz/75 g) light corn syrup
2 teaspoons finely grated lemon zest
2 tablespoons fresh lemon juice
1 teaspoon vanilla extract (essence)
⅛ teaspoon salt
2 cups (16 fl oz/500 ml) low-fat
   buttermilk

This sherbet will surprise you: It's rich tasting and similar in flavor to cheesecake, yet is almost fat free. Any variety of peach can be used as long as the fruit is ripe and sweet. To make a plain version with a hint of lemon, omit the fruit and reduce the sugar to ⅓ cup (3 oz/90 g).

*I*f using peaches, bring a saucepan three-fourths full of water to a boil. Immerse the peaches in the water for 30 seconds, then, using a slotted spoon, transfer to a work surface. When cool enough to handle, slip off the skins. Halve and pit the peaches, then cut into chunks. If using strawberries, remove the stems.

In a food processor fitted with the metal blade or in a blender, combine the peaches or strawberries, sugar, corn syrup, lemon zest, lemon juice, vanilla and salt. Purée until smooth, then pour the mixture into a large, shallow bowl. Stir in the buttermilk.

Cover the bowl and place in a freezer. As the sherbet begins to freeze, after about 1½ hours, beat it vigorously with a whisk. Re-cover and return to the freezer. Continue to beat the sherbet every hour or so until it is fully frozen; this will help make it smooth. It should take 4–6 hours in all, or possibly longer, depending upon the temperature of the freezer. The sherbet can also be frozen in an ice cream maker; follow the manufacturer's instructions.

Makes about 5 cups (40 fl oz/1.25 l); serves 8

*Nutritional Analysis
Per Serving:*

Calories 149
(Kilojoules 626)
Protein 3 g
Carbohydrates 34 g
Total Fat 1 g
Saturated Fat 1 g
Cholesterol 4 mg
Sodium 78 mg
Dietary Fiber 1 g

Chocolate Angel Food Cake

¾ cup (3 oz/90 g) cake (soft-wheat)
   flour
¼ cup (¾ oz/20 g) unsweetened cocoa
1½ cups (12 oz/370 g) granulated sugar
2 cups (16 fl oz/500 ml) egg whites
   (12–14)
1½ teaspoons cream of tartar
½ teaspoon salt
2 teaspoons vanilla extract (essence)
confectioners' (icing) sugar, optional
strawberry or peach slices, optional

*P*reheat an oven to 350°F (180°C).

Sift together the cake flour, the cocoa and ¾ cup (6 oz/185 g) of the granulated sugar onto a sheet of waxed paper. Repeat the sifting 2 more times. Set aside.

Put the egg whites in a large bowl. Using an electric mixer set on low speed, beat just until foamy on top, about 30 seconds. Add the cream of tartar, salt and vanilla; increase the speed to medium and beat until the whites have increased to about 5 times their original volume and have formed a foamy white mass that is still quite soft and flattens out when you stop beating.

Continuing to beat, gradually add the remaining ¾ cup (6 oz/ 185 g) granulated sugar, taking about 15 seconds to incorporate it. Then beat until the whites form a shiny, voluminous mass of very tiny bubbles. They should barely hold their shape when the beater is lifted, and slide when the bowl is tilted.

Sift the flour-cocoa mixture over the whites, then, using a rubber spatula, gently and quickly fold it in, just until there are no unblended drifts of flour. Pour the batter into an ungreased 10-inch (25-cm) angel food or tube pan and tap the pan firmly but gently on the counter once or twice to settle the batter.

Bake until the cake has risen to the top of the pan, or higher, and a thin wooden skewer inserted into the center comes out clean, 45–55 minutes. Remove from the oven. Invert the pan; if it doesn't have legs around the top rim, place the tube over an inverted metal funnel or the neck of a bottle for support. Cool upside down for at least 2 hours, or longer.

To remove the cake from the pan, run a long metal icing spatula between the cake and the pan. Gently ease the cake out of the pan onto a serving plate. Dust the top with confectioners' sugar, if desired. Cut into wedges to serve and accompany with sliced fruit, if desired.

Makes one 10-inch (25-cm) cake; serves 10

*NUTRITIONAL ANALYSIS
PER SERVING:*

CALORIES 196
(KILOJOULES 823)
PROTEIN 6 G
CARBOHYDRATES 43 G
TOTAL FAT 0 G
SATURATED FAT 0 G
CHOLESTEROL 0 MG
SODIUM 190 MG
DIETARY FIBER 1 G

Lemon Ice with Berry Sauce

2¼ cups (18 fl oz/560 ml) water
1½ cups (12 oz/375 g) sugar
2 tablespoons finely grated lemon zest
⅔ cup (5 fl oz/160 ml) fresh lemon
  juice
1 cup (8 fl oz/250 ml) orange marmalade-
  raspberry sauce *(recipe on page 13)*
fresh mint sprigs

The combination of crystalline ice and red berry sauce is stunning. For a creamier, sherbetlike consistency, add ¼ cup (2 fl oz/ 60 ml) sweetened condensed milk to the mixture before freezing.

*I*n a saucepan over high heat, combine the water and sugar. When the mixture begins to boil, stir it a few times to make sure the sugar is fully dissolved, then boil without stirring for 2 minutes. Remove from the heat, add the lemon zest and pour the mixture into a large, shallow bowl. Let cool, then stir in the lemon juice.

Cover the bowl and place in a freezer. As the mixture begins to freeze, after about 1½ hours, beat it vigorously with a wire whisk. Re-cover and return to the freezer. Continue to beat every hour or so until it is fully frozen; this will help make it smooth. It should take about 4 hours in all, or possibly longer, depending upon the temperature of the freezer.

Meanwhile, make the orange marmalade–raspberry sauce.

To serve, scoop the ice onto individual plates and pour about 2½ tablespoons of the orange marmalade–raspberry sauce over each serving. Garnish with mint sprigs and serve at once.

Makes about 1 qt (1 l); serves 6

Nutritional Analysis Per Serving:

Calories 310
(Kilojoules 1,302)
Protein 1 g
Carbohydrates 81 g
Total Fat 0 g
Saturated Fat 0 g
Cholesterol 0 mg
Sodium 12 mg
Dietary Fiber 2 g

Peach Halves with Crumbly Topping

⅔ cup (3 oz/90 g) all-purpose (plain) flour

⅔ cup (5 oz/155 g) firmly packed brown sugar

⅔ cup (2 oz/60 g) regular or quick-cooking rolled oats

3 tablespoons unsalted butter, at room temperature, cut into pieces

½ teaspoon ground nutmeg

¼ teaspoon salt

6 large firm, ripe freestone peaches

2 tablespoons brandy, rum or fresh lemon juice

Here, peaches are baked with a delectable brown sugar and rolled oats topping, resulting in a dessert much like a fruit crisp.

Preheat an oven to 350°F (180°C). Coat an 8-inch (20-cm) square cake pan or a 9-inch (23-cm) round pie pan with nonstick cooking spray.

In a bowl, combine the flour, brown sugar, rolled oats, butter, nutmeg and salt. Using your fingers or a pastry blender, rub or cut the butter into the dry ingredients until the mixture is crumbly; set aside.

Halve the peaches and remove their pits. It is not necessary to peel them unless you wish to do so. (If you do, see the recipe on page 92 for the technique.) Place the peaches, cut sides up, in a single layer in the prepared pan. Drizzle with the liquor or lemon juice and then sprinkle evenly with the oat topping.

Bake until the topping has browned and the peaches are tender when pierced with the tip of a sharp knife, 25–30 minutes. Remove from the oven and let cool briefly, then serve warm.

Serves 4

Nutritional Analysis Per Serving:

Calories 455
(Kilojoules 1,911)
Protein 6 g
Carbohydrates 84 g
Total Fat 10 g
Saturated Fat 6 g
Cholesterol 23 mg
Sodium 150 mg
Dietary Fiber 6 g

Autumn Fruit Compote

3 cups (24 fl oz/750 ml) water
½ cup (4 oz/125 g) sugar
2 tablespoons fresh lemon juice
1 cinnamon stick, 3 inches (7.5 cm) long
2 quinces
2 firm, ripe pears, preferably Bosc
2 apples, preferably Golden Delicious
1 cup (6 oz/185 g) pitted prunes
1 teaspoon vanilla extract (essence)

Quinces, which look like pale yellow apples, are harsh tasting and tough when raw. Stewing them in a sweetened liquid brings out their unique spicy flavor and turns the flesh from yellow to an appealing pale pink. Even in season, quinces can be hard to find. If unavailable, substitute additional apples or pears. Serve this fruit compote for breakfast, brunch or dessert. It is good warm or cold.

*I*n a large saucepan, combine the water, sugar, lemon juice and cinnamon stick. Bring to a boil over high heat, stirring to dissolve the sugar. Reduce the heat to low, cover and cook gently while you prepare the fruit.

Peel, halve and core the quinces. Cut each half into 4 wedges. Drop the quinces into the liquid and simmer, covered, for 15 minutes. Meanwhile, peel, halve and core the pears and apples. Cut each half into 4 wedges. Add the pears, apples and prunes to the pan and continue to simmer, covered, until the fresh fruits are tender but not mushy and the prunes are plump, 10–15 minutes longer.

Remove from the heat, stir in the vanilla and set aside for at least 30 minutes before serving.

Serves 6

Nutritional Analysis Per Serving:

Calories 222
(Kilojoules 932)
Protein 1 g
Carbohydrates 58 g
Total Fat 1 g
Saturated Fat 0 g
Cholesterol 0 mg
Sodium 3 mg
Dietary Fiber 4 g

Cold Raspberry-Yogurt Soufflé

2 envelopes (2½ teaspoons each)
  unflavored gelatin
⅔ cup (5 fl oz/160 ml) water
4 cups (1 lb/500 g) raspberries
¾ cup (6 oz/185 g) sugar
¼ cup (2 fl oz/60 ml) tequila or raspberry liqueur, optional
5 egg whites
pinch of salt
1 cup (8 oz/250 g) nonfat plain yogurt,
  stirred until smooth

In a small saucepan, sprinkle the gelatin over ⅓ cup (2½ fl oz/ 80 ml) of the water, stir and let stand for several minutes to soften.

In a food processor fitted with the metal blade or in a blender, combine the raspberries and the remaining ⅓ cup (2½ fl oz/80 ml) water and purée until smooth. Strain the purée through a fine-mesh sieve set over a large bowl to remove the seeds, pressing the purée with the back of a wooden spoon. Stir ½ cup (4 oz/ 125 g) of the sugar into the purée and set aside.

Place the saucepan with the softened gelatin over low heat and stir just until the gelatin granules have dissolved and the liquid is clear, about 2 minutes. Watch carefully and do not allow to boil. Add the dissolved gelatin and tequila or liqueur to the berry purée and whisk to mix thoroughly. Cover and refrigerate, stirring occasionally, until the mixture is chilled and has thickened slightly, 1–2 hours.

Meanwhile, prepare a soufflé dish or nonreactive cylindrical mold of 1 qt (32 fl oz/1 l) capacity. Cut a sheet of waxed paper long enough to encircle the mold, and fold it in half lengthwise. Wrap the waxed paper snugly around the top of the mold so that a "collar" extends about 3 inches (7.5 cm) above the rim. Tape the paper securely in place.

In a large bowl, using an electric mixer set at medium to medium-high speed, beat the egg whites with the salt until soft peaks form. Add the remaining ¼ cup (2 oz/60 g) sugar and continue to beat until stiff peaks form. Add the yogurt and, using a rubber spatula, gently stir into the whites. Scoop the berry mixture on top of the whites and, using the spatula, fold in just until no white streaks remain.

Pour into the prepared dish or mold. Refrigerate for at least 6 hours or as long as overnight. Remove the collar just before taking the chilled soufflé to the table.

Serves 8

*Nutritional Analysis
Per Serving:*

Calories 142
(Kilojoules 596)
Protein 6 g
Carbohydrates 30 g
Total Fat 0 g
Saturated Fat 0 g
Cholesterol 0 mg
Sodium 76 mg
Dietary Fiber 3 g

Glossary

The following glossary defines terms specifically as they relate to healthy cooking, including major and unusual ingredients and basic techniques.

APPLES

Low in calories and abundant in dietary fiber, apples are an excellent healthy dessert ingredient, as well as a sharp, sweet flavor addition to savory dishes. Among the most popular and widely available are Granny Smith, a green Australian variety ideal for cooking; pippins, green to yellow-green fruits with a slightly tart taste suited to salads or cooking; the red, slightly tart Rome Beauty, ideal for baking or eating raw; and the crisp, light and juicy Golden Delicious.

To core an apple, use an apple corer, a sharp-edged metal tube that presses down easily through the center of the fruit to remove the core, a task that should precede peeling if the fruit is to be cooked and served whole. Use a swivel-bladed vegetable peeler or a small, sharp knife to remove the peel.

To prevent peeled or cored apples from discoloring, toss with lemon juice.

ASPARAGUS

A favorite vegetable of springtime, asparagus is low in calories and high in vitamin C. Seek out spears that appear fresh, firm and crisp, with compact tips—the most tender 2–5 inches (5–13 cm) of the budding ends, prized for their delicate flavor and texture.

To prepare asparagus for cooking, cut or snap off any tough, woody ends. Starting about 2 inches (5 cm) below the tip, use a vegetable peeler to remove the thin, tough outer skin to the stem end.

BELL PEPPERS

Also known as capsicums, these sweet-fleshed, bell-shaped members of the pepper family are an outstanding source of vitamin C; they also provide some vitamin B$_6$, and the ripe, red variety is rich in vitamin A.

To prepare a raw bell pepper, cut lengthwise in halves or quarters with a sharp knife. Pull out the stem section from each piece, along with the cluster of seeds attached to it. Remove any remaining seeds and any thin white membranes, or ribs, to which they are attached. Cut the pepper halves as called for in individual recipes.

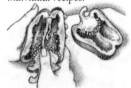

When a recipe calls for roasted bell peppers, preheat a broiler (griller) and line a broiler pan with aluminum foil. Prepare pepper quarters as directed above and place cut sides down on the pan. Broil (grill) about 4 inches (10 cm) below the heat source until the skins are evenly blackened and blistered, 5–6 minutes. Remove from the broiler. Cover with aluminum foil; let stand for 10 minutes, then peel away the skins.

BULGUR

Wheat berries that have been parboiled, dried, partially debranned and cracked into coarse particles, bulgur is remarkable for its nutlike taste and chewy texture. Low in fat and sodium, and rich in complex carbohydrates and fiber, it is sold in shops specializing in Middle Eastern foods, in health-food stores and in well-stocked food stores. Also known as burghul.

BUTTERMILK

Although its name gives the impression of richness, buttermilk, originally the liquid residue produced in the churning of butter, is today commonly skim milk to which bacterial cultures are added; it is therefore low in fat. It contributes tanginess and a thick, creamy texture to recipes, as well as an acidity that provides a boost to leavening agents such as baking soda (bicarbonate of soda) in baked goods. Fat percentages vary from product to product, so check nutritional labels in search of those with approximately 1 percent fat by volume, deriving 20 percent or fewer total calories from fat.

CHEESES

Although cheeses in general are fairly high in fat, they are also excellent sources of protein, calcium and vitamin B$_{12}$. Careful shopping will lead to types with generally lower fat content. Cottage cheese, a rich-tasting curd cheese, is sold in both large- and small-curd forms, with the latter blending more easily into recipe mixtures. Parmesan is fairly rich, with 59 percent of its calories coming from fat. However, this thick-crusted, aged Italian cow's milk cheese has a sharp, salty, full flavor, which means that a little

goes a long way in seasoning recipes. Buy in block form, to grate fresh as needed. The finest Italian variety is designated Parmigiano-Reggiano®.

COUSCOUS

Steamed like a grain and served with stews, couscous, a North African specialty, is actually tiny, pasta pellets made from semolina wheat, rich in carbohydrates. Products labeled "quick cooking," found in well-stocked food stores, have been precooked and redried, and are prepared in a fraction of the time required by the long-cooking variety.

EGGPLANTS

Vegetable-fruit, also known as aubergine, with tender, mildly earthy, sweet flesh. The shiny skins of eggplants vary in color from purple to red and from yellow to white, and their shapes range from small and oval to long and slender to large and pearlike. The most common variety is the large, purple globe eggplant. Slender, purple Asian eggplants (below), more tender and with fewer, smaller seeds, are available with increasing frequency in food stores and vegetable markets.

EGGS

Although relatively low in calories and rich in protein, eggs are high in fat and cholesterol. They should be eaten in moderation or, whenever possible, only their fat-free whites—separated from the rich yolks—should be used.

To separate an egg, crack the shell in half by tapping it against the side of a bowl and then breaking it apart with your fingers. Holding the shell halves over the bowl, gently transfer the whole yolk back and forth between them, letting the clear white drop away into the bowl. Take care not to break the yolk (the whites will not beat properly if they contain any yolk). Transfer the yolk to another bowl.

The same basic function is also performed by an aluminum, ceramic or plastic egg separator placed over a bowl. The separator holds the yolk intact in its cuplike center while allowing the white to drip out through one or more slots in its side into the bowl.

GARLIC

This bulb—popular worldwide as a seasoning, both raw and cooked—has been found to thin the blood and lower the cholesterol levels of those who eat it regularly. For the best flavor, purchase whole heads of dry garlic, separating individual cloves from the head as needed; it is best not to purchase more than you will use in 1 or 2 weeks, as garlic can shrivel and lose its flavor with prolonged storage.

To peel a garlic clove, place on a work surface and cover with the side of a large chef's knife. Press firmly but carefully on the side of the knife to crush the clove slightly; the dry skin will slip off easily.

MILK

Whole milk is high in calories and fat and is highly nutritious. Milk products from which some or all of the fat has been removed are still good sources of protein, calcium and vitamins A, D and B$_{12}$. When buying low-fat milk, check whether the product is labeled 2 percent or 1 percent; the latter derives less of its calories from fat than the former. Canned evaporated milk is milk from which approximately 60 percent of the water has been removed, resulting in an intensified flavor and consistency that enriches some desserts and cream sauces; seek out evaporated milk made from low-fat or nonfat milk.

MUSHROOMS

The meaty texture and rich, earthy flavor of cultivated mushrooms belie the fact that they are low in calories, almost totally lacking in fat, and good sources of fiber, complex carbohydrates and minerals. They are widely available in food markets and greengrocers; in their smallest form, with their caps still closed, they are often called button mushrooms (above, right).

To clean fresh mushrooms, brush away dirt from their surface with a soft-bristled mushroom brush, or a lightly dampened kitchen or paper towel. Do not rinse them, as they easily absorb water.

NONSTICK COOKING SPRAY

This pressurized mixture of oil, lecithin (an emulsifier derived from soybeans), sometimes grain alcohol, and a harmless propellant is used to coat cooking surfaces while adding very little fat to finished dishes.

HERBS

All kinds of dried and fresh herbs are used to add vibrant flavor to foods without an increase in calories or fat. Herbs used in this book include:

Bay leaves

Dried whole leaves of the bay laurel tree. Pungent and spicy, they flavor simmered dishes, marinades and pickling mixtures. The French variety, sometimes available in specialty-food shops, has a milder, sweeter flavor than California bay leaves. Discard the leaves before serving.

Chives

Long, thin green shoots (below) with a mild flavor reminiscent of the onion, to which they are related. Although chives are available dried in the herb-and-spice section of food stores, fresh chives possess the best flavor.

Cilantro

Green, leafy herb (below) resembling **flat-leaf (Italian) parsley,** with a sharp, aromatic, somewhat astringent flavor. Popular in Latin American and Asian cuisines. Also called fresh coriander or Chinese parsley.

Italian Mixed Herbs

Commercial dried herb blends, which may include such Italian favorites as basil, oregano, **rosemary** and **parsley.**

Parsley

This popular fresh herb is available in two main varieties, the curly-leaf type and a flat-leaf type. The latter, also known as Italian parsley (below), has a more pronounced flavor and is preferred.

Rosemary

Mediterranean herb, used fresh (below) or dried, with an aromatic flavor particularly well suited to poultry, lamb and veal. Strong in flavor, it should be used sparingly, except when grilling.

Sage

Pungent herb, used fresh (below) or dried, that marries well with fresh or cured pork, lamb, veal and poultry.

Tarragon

Fragrant, distinctively sweet herb used fresh or dried as a seasoning for salads, seafood, chicken, light meats, eggs and vegetables.

OILS

Used as an ingredient, to conduct heat and prevent sticking during cooking, and to lubricate pans for baking, oils are simply fats—derived from seeds, plants, nuts, fruits, legumes—that are liquid at room temperature. Being virtually pure fat, they should be avoided in excess in a healthy diet; used judiciously, they can subtly enhance the flavor of recipes in which they are included, as well as add generous amounts of vitamin E.

Sesame oils from China and Japan are commonly made with roasted sesame seeds, resulting in dark, strong-tasting oils generally used as a flavoring; their low smoking point makes them unsuitable for using alone as a cooking medium.

Olive oil is prized for its pure, fruity taste and golden to pale green hue.

Safflower, canola and other high-quality mild vegetable oils are used when a relatively flavorless oil is desired.

Walnut oil, popular in dressings and as a seasoning, conveys the rich taste of the nuts from which it is pressed. Oil made from lightly toasted nuts has a full but not overly assertive flavor.

PARSNIPS

Root vegetables similar in shape and texture to carrots, parsnips have ivory flesh and an appealingly sweet flavor. They carry complex carbohydrates and fiber, as well as folic acid, potassium and magnesium.

PEARS

All pear varieties are rich in fiber and contain vitamin C, folic acid and potassium. Bosc pears (below), which are good cooking pears, are long, slender, tapered, autumn-to-winter fruits with yellow-and-russet skin and slightly grainy, solid-textured white flesh with a hint of acidity. Bartlett pears, also called Williams' pears, are shaped roughly like bells, with creamy yellow skins sometimes tinged in red; fine textured, juicy and mild tasting, they are equally good for cooking or eating and are available from summer to early autumn.

POLENTA

Italian term both for a cooked mush of specially ground cornmeal and for the cornmeal itself. Sometimes enriched with butter, cream, cheese or eggs, polenta has an earthy, satisfying flavor when served unembellished. Like all cornmeal, it is high in fiber and low in fat and is a good source of magnesium, iron, thiamin and niacin.

RICE

Low in fat and high in complex carbohydrates, rice is a highly nutritious grain. Brown rice, the whole grain with only its tough outer husk removed, is the most nutritious choice, providing fiber, magnesium, vitamin B_6 and other nutrients; white rice, milled to remove its bran, has less fiber and, unless labeled enriched, fewer nutrients. Arborio rice, a popular Italian white variety with short, round grains, has a high starch content that creates a creamy, saucelike consistency during cooking; it is available in Italian delicatessens and well-stocked food stores. Medium-grain rice shares some of the characteristics of both long-grain and short-grain rice, cooking to a fluffy texture like the former but tending to clump together like the latter.

RUTABAGAS

These roots, among the cancer-combating cruciferous vegetables, resemble large turnips, with sweet, pale yellow-orange flesh. They are notably high in vitamin C. Also known as swedes.

SCALLOPS, SEA

Large variety of the bivalve mollusk with rounds of flesh about 1½ inches (4 cm) in diameter. Usually sold already shelled, fresh scallops may sometimes be found still in their shell, complete with their sweet-flavored, orange-pink corals attached. Scallops are low in fat, relatively low in cholesterol and exceptionally high in vitamin B_{12}; they also contain some of the heart-healthy omega-3 fatty acids.

SHRIMP

This popular shellfish is low in fat and high in vitamin B_{12}. Raw shrimp (prawns) are generally sold with the heads already removed but the shells still intact. Before cooking, they are usually peeled and their thin, veinlike intestinal tracts are removed.

To peel and devein shrimp, use your thumbs to split open the thin shell along the concave side, between the two rows of legs. Grasp the shell and gently peel it away.

Using a small knife, make a shallow slit along the back of the shrimp, just deep enough to expose the long, usually dark, veinlike intestinal tract. With the tip of the knife or your fingers, lift up and pull out the vein and discard.

PASTA

Complex carbohydrate-rich pastas of many shapes and sizes star as main courses and side dishes in healthy diets. Hundreds of distinct commercial pasta shapes exist. Some of the more common ones, used in this book, include:

Fettuccine
"Ribbons." Popular in both egg and spinach varieties.

Linguine
"Small tongues." Long, narrow, flat strands.

Manicotti
"Muffs." Large tubes for stuffing.

Orzo
Small, rice-shaped pasta.

Penne
"Quills." Tubes of regular or spinach pasta with angled ends resembling pen nibs. Available smooth and ridged (rigate).

Rigatoni
Moderately sized ridged tubes.

Spaghetti
Classic long rods.

SOY SAUCE

Asian seasoning and condiment made from soybeans, wheat, salt and water. Seek out good-quality imported soy sauces; Chinese brands tend to be saltier than Japanese. Varieties labeled "low or reduced sodium," while still fairly high in salt, offer a somewhat healthier alternative.

SPINACH

Rich in vitamins, minerals and fiber, this leafy green vegetable may be eaten raw in salads or cooked. Choose smaller, more tender spinach leaves if possible. Be sure to wash thoroughly to eliminate all dirt and sand: Put the spinach leaves in a sink or large basin and fill with cold water to cover generously. Agitate the leaves in the water to remove their dirt, then lift the leaves out of the water and set aside. Drain the sink or basin thoroughly, rinsing well. Repeat the procedure until no grit remains.

STOCK

Flavorful liquid derived from slowly simmering chicken, meat, fish or vegetables in water, along with herbs, spices and aromatic vegetables. Used as the primary cooking liquid or moistening and flavoring agent in many recipes. Stock may be made fairly easily at home, to be frozen for future use; take special care to skim off fat from its surface before using. Many good-quality canned broths or stocks, in regular or concentrated form, are also available; they tend to be saltier than homemade stock, however, so recipes in which they are used should be carefully tasted for seasoning. Seek out brands whose labels indicate they are lower in sodium and fat. Excellent stocks may also be found in the freezer section of quality food stores. Clam juice, the refreshingly briny strained liquid of shucked clams, is often used in place of seafood stock; it is sold in small bottles in the fresh or canned seafood departments of food stores.

TOMATOES

During summer, when tomatoes are in season, use the best red or yellow sun-ripened tomatoes you can find. At other times of year, plum tomatoes, sometimes called Roma or egg tomatoes, are likely to have the best flavor and texture. For cooking, canned plum tomatoes are also good.

To peel fresh tomatoes, first bring a saucepan three-fourths full of water to a boil. Using a small, sharp knife, cut out the core from the stem end of each tomato, and cut a shallow X in the skin at the tomato's base. Submerge for about 20 seconds in the boiling water, then remove and dip in a bowl of cold water. Starting at the X, peel the skin from the tomato, using your fingertips and, if necessary, the knife blade (below).

Cut the tomatoes as directed in individual recipes.

To seed a tomato (below), cut it in half crosswise. Squeeze gently to force out the seed sacs.

Sun-dried tomatoes (below) have an intense, sweet-tart flavor and a pleasantly chewy texture that enhance savory recipes. For low-fat cooking, use only those that have been packed dry, avoiding those in oil.

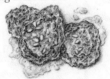

Tomato paste is a commercial concentrate of puréed tomatoes, commonly sold in small cans, used to add flavor and body to sauces; imported tubes of double-strength tomato concentrate, sold in Italian delicatessens and well-stocked food stores, have a superior flavor.

TURNIPS

Small, creamy white root vegetables, tinged purple or green at the crown, with firm, pungent yet slightly sweet flesh, turnips provide good quantities of vitamin C along with dietary fiber. Generally cooked by boiling, braising or stewing. Choose smaller turnips that feel heavy for their size and are firm to the touch.

YOGURT

Milk fermented by bacterial cultures that impart a mildly acidic flavor and custardlike texture, yogurt is an excellent source of protein, calcium and vitamin B_{12}. So-called plain yogurt refers to the unflavored product, to distinguish it from the many popular types of flavored and sweetened yogurt on the market. Available made from whole, low-fat or nonfat milk.

ZEST

The thin, brightly colored, outermost layer of a citrus fruit's peel, zest contains most of its aromatic essential oils—a lively source of flavor in both savory and sweet recipes. Zest may be removed by one of two easy methods:

Use a simple tool known as a zester, drawing its sharp-edged holes across the fruit's skin to remove the zest in thin strips.

Holding the edge of a paring knife or vegetable peeler away from you and almost parallel to the fruit's skin, carefully cut off the zest in thin strips, taking care not to remove any of the bitter white pith with it. Then thinly slice or chop the strips on a cutting board.

Index

ACKNOWLEDGMENTS

The publishers would like to thank the following people for their generous assistance and support in producing this book: Stephen W. Griswold, Sharon C. Lott, Ken DellaPenta, Tina Schmitz, Ruth Jacobson, the buyers and store managers for Pottery Barn and Williams-Sonoma stores.

The following kindly lent props for the photography: American Rag-Maison, Biordi Art Imports, Candelier, Fillamento, Forrest Jones, RH Shop, Sue Fisher King, Chuck Williams, Williams-Sonoma, Pottery Barn.